WAR DIARIES

Published by Brolga Publishing Pty Ltd
ABN 46 063 962 443
PO Box 12544
A'Beckett St
Melbourne, VIC, 8006
Australia

email: markzocchi@brolgapublishing.com.au

National Library of Australia
Cataloguing-in-Publication data

Lasslett, Frederick William, 1918 –
Australian War Diaries of a Japanese P.O.W.
ISBN 9781922036551

Printed in China
Cover design by David Khan
Typeset by Wanissa Somsuphangsri

WAR DIARIES

FRED LASSLETT

This book is dedicated to Nola,
and my fellow shipmates of the HMAS Perth
who died in action
or died in the POW camps.

CONTENTS

FOREWORD

A few words are offered here to set the scene for the pages from my War Diaries that follow.

My time in the RAN commenced as follows:

I enlisted in the Royal Australian Navy on 22nd April 1937 at HMAS Lonsdale at Port Melbourne as a Reservist. I attended once a week from 5pm - 9pm and studied to be a wireless-telegraphist. My official number was PM 1848. Because of a break in attendance due to working shift work at Olympic Tyres, I was discharged for unsatisfactory attendance on 8th June 1939.

On 1st September 1939, German troops invaded Poland. Britain and France sent ultimatums to Hitler demanding his withdrawal from Poland. Hitler declined to respond. On September 3, Prime Minister Chamberlain went to the airwaves to announce to the British people that a state of war existed between their country and Germany. World War II had begun.

I was called up on 21st September 1940, and ordered to attend HMAS Cerberus (Flinders Naval Base). I was in a group of approximately 40 and we were asked by a Chief Petty Officer whether any of us had previous defence force service. I stated that I had previous service as a wireless-telegraphist at HMAS Lonsdale.

On board HMAS Perth, in the Middle East, when the
Australian Broadcasting Commission's field unit was
making a recording of the men's voices for a
broadcast to Australia.

After being equipped with uniforms and being medically
tested, I was ordered to be in charge of drilling the men on
the parade ground with normal military exercises such as
left turn, right turn, etc. for two hours. I wore a gold crown
on my left sleeve as a badge of authority.

This went on for a week, and then the men went to
different classes as ordinary seamen, torpedo, engine
room and gunnery. On learning that I attended night
school at the Melbourne Institute of Engineering to study

to be an electrical mechanic, I was ordered to attend class to be an Electrical Wireman (Electrical Repair Party) because of the shortage of electricians in the navy.

After 6 weeks training on the electrical set-up of navy ships, I was invested with the badge of wireman and included in the torpedo section.

I was promoted to Class Captain and on 4th October, with temporary rank of Naval Police, I was ordered to escort 43 naval ratings to Fremantle by train with a naval Lieutenant. We arrived at Fremantle and were billeted at HMAS Leeuwin Depot. After a week there, on 14th November, we were transferred to HMAS Perth.

After several convoy duties from Fremantle to Ceylon, we eventually arrived at Alexandria, Egypt in December 1940.

Our first air attack by German planes was at Suda Bay, Crete. We were anchored in a gorge and we opened up with 6" and 4" shells, and the result was one barn, two dead cows.

An article in an Australian newspaper during June 1941 covered the evacuation of troops and civilians from Crete:

HMAS Perth took part in the greatest battle of all times, staged north of Crete last week.

It culminated last Thursday when the Germans flung in at least 500 bombers, subjecting the Navy to an incessant 15-hour attack.

Warship guns blazed all day long until the red hot air was filled with the scream of bombs, the roar of planes, crashing of shells and blasting of pom-poms.

www.awm.gov.au   P01915.008

At sea, off Crete, circa. 21-05-1941. Water sprays into the air from the impact of 1000lb bombs falling in the sea near HMAS Perth during the evacuation of Australian soldiers from Greece. Seen from HMAS Perth. (Donor: I. Futcher)

Britain lost two cruisers, the Gloucester and Fiji, and four destroyers Juno, Kelly, Greyhound and Kashmir. About 1000 men have been saved.

Lord Louis Mountbatten, cousin of the King, was Captain of the Greyhound. It is believed he was rescued.

In that battle, we survived an incredible 257 direct air attacks.

Our port was Alexandria in Egypt, and at dusk the German aircraft would drop sea mines by parachute. These mines looked like 40-gallon oil drums and would submerge just beneath the sea. Most times they were shot down by shells from our ships. When we saw them dropping by parachute, I imagine everybody thought they were going to land on their ship.

One amazing sight was the firing of missiles from a French cruiser. From what I was told, these missiles consisted of chicken wire and explosives which were alight in the air. I think the idea was that the chicken wire would wrap around the planes' propellers.

We continued doing convoy duties to Tobruk, Malta and Greece.

While we were in Valletta harbour in Malta, a German

plane dropped a stick of bombs on the terrace houses along the docks, and one bomb down the funnel of a merchant ship berthed behind us. The ship caught fire, and as a member of the Electrical Repair Party, I assisted the other crewmembers to bring the dead and wounded to the shore and put out the fire. We were informed later that the ship was carrying ammunition. We were very lucky that the ship never exploded.

Malta, 06-01-1941. HMS Illustrious and HMAS Perth under German air attack in Grand Harbour, during which the Illustrious, under repairs from damage sustained in convoy duties, was again hit.
The Perth received underwater and internal damage, but no casualties from a near miss.

Our next main event was the Battle of Matapan. HMAS Perth, one of the units of Sir Andrew Cunningham's fleet which established control in the Mediterranean, played a notable part in the battle of Cape Matapan on March 28–29, in which the Italians lost three heavy cruisers and two destroyers, and probably a six-inch gun cruiser and a large destroyer.

The battle was recorded in the Australian newspapers on August 15 1941, after the Perth returned to Sydney:

A dramatic story of ordeal under dive bombing and high level bombing, of action against the Italian Fleet at Matapan, and of evacuation from Greece and Crete is told by the officers and men of an Australian warship which has returned to Australian waters. The vessel served for six months in the Mediterranean. In that period, many hundreds of bombs were aimed at her, but she was hit only once.

The cruiser played a part in the Battle of Matapan; she helped in the bombardment of the Libyan coast, took off hundreds of men from Greece and Crete, and bombarded Vichy forces on the Syrian coast.

Four of her complement were decorated for gallantry in fighting a fire which broke out in an ammunition ship lying 30 feet away from her stern in Malta Harbour. They were Lieut. CJP Guille, who was awarded the OBE and Leading-Stokers PG Allon and PP Larmer, and Canteen-Manager ATR Hawkins, who were awarded the British Empire Medal.

www.awm.gov.au

P01915.004

Matapan, Greece, 28-03-1941. Smoke screens forward
of HMAS Perth during the Battle of Matapan.
Seen from HMAS Perth.
(Donor I. Futcher)

Even after battles you notice the strange events that occur.
During the time when the German planes scored a hit on
the ammunition ship which was anchored behind us, one
bomb demolished a row of tenant houses, and one terrace
house had three of its walls demolished, but the remaining wall was left undamaged and a painting of the Virgin
Mary was still hanging on the wall.

Another remarkable incident was seeing the Maltese
fishermen picking up the fish that had been stunned by the
explosions.

And thirdly, a 2000-pound bomb landed in the latrines situated on the wharf. The bomb did not explode, and 2 or 3 feet protruded through the roof, and later there was a notice placed on the building "Unsafe to enter".

Mediterranean Area, 1941. Some crew members of HMAS Perth astride one of the ship's big guns.

Later on, about October 1941, we arrived in Sydney for a refit.

After the refit, we sailed to Fremantle and commenced convoying duties to Ceylon.

FOREWORD

On our return from Ceylon, we berthed at Fremantle where we were told of the sinking of HMAS Sydney by an armed merchant ship, Kormoran, on 19 November 1941. We set sail to find this armed merchant ship, and sighted a merchant ship. We went to battle stations, and when the merchant ship refused to stop we fired a six-inch shell across its bow. It soon stopped. The merchant ship was a Portuguese ship and could not find its codebook to answer our signal.

In February we set sail for Java, Indonesia, arriving at Surabaya on 24th February 1942.

THE DIARIES

The following letters, for the period 23-2-42 to 11-1-43, were written by Fred Lasslett, in pencil, into a small exercise book, which was concealed from the Japanese.

F W Lasslett O N 24566

Dear Nola,

Whilst on this island of Java as a prisoner of war, I dedicate these weekly letters to the ever-fresh and beautiful memories of you.

I met Nola at a dance at the Brunswick Town Hall. She was a singer for the band, and during her break I asked her for a dance. During the week, she had a hairdressing shop. We went out together over the next three or four months before I was called up.

THE LAST DAYS OF HMAS PERTH

HMAS Perth in Sydney harbour

23rd February 1942

Dear Nola,

Once again the good old ship has left the sunny shores of Australia for another destination unknown (14-2-1942).

Later the same day, our destination was announced as Batavia, a city of Java. The feelings of the crew were mixed. The ratings that had recently joined the ship cheered like mad, for it meant possibly their first naval action, whilst the older ratings, including yours truly, were rather dubious about the outcome of this voyage.

With the experiences of the Mediterranean still fresh in our memory and realising that Japan most likely had a large naval fleet around those parts, we guessed that we all would be in for a hot time before we eventually arrived back in Australia.

The voyage was uneventful, though when we approached the Straits of Sunda, which divide Java from Sumatra, we had a scare when the outlines of ships were seen on our starboard beam. Luckily they turned out to be a friendly convoy. When we saw those ships, I sure wished I was with you.

Early the following morning we sailed into the Port of Batavia. As you approach Batavia, you are struck by the freshness and colouring of the city. With the cool greenery of the jungle, with the wavering coconut trees towering in the air and a beautiful sunset which would delight the soul of the most hardened artist, this Java is like an emerald of the sea. Gosh, I'm going all romantic about this.

To continue, we berthed at 0830 hrs on the 24th February, and at 2000 hrs that night I went ashore.

As time is short, I'll continue this in the next letter.

Love Fred xx

24th February 1942

Dear Nola,

To continue, I went ashore at 2000 hrs that night and as the leave was only to 2200 hrs, I never had time to travel to Batavia proper.

Owing to the place being blacked-out there wasn't much to see. The natives were similar to any other island native, dirty, smelly and unclean. The place being more of a village than a town, there weren't any modern shops or theatres, so I wandered down to the market.

At the market, my outstanding impressions are of the babble of sound, the smell, and variety of things for sale. You can buy anything from beautiful lace work, jewels, all kinds of native fruit and a large variety of tobacco and cigarettes.

Everything was cheap, especially tobacco. A packet of Silver City cigarettes, which cost 2/6d back home, cost only 4 pence. A Guilder is worth 3/8d therefore 5 cents is roughly 2 pence (tuppence).

Whilst at the market, I bought a few trinkets and a handbag made of native flax-like grass.

As time was near for me to go back to my ship, I bought a few apples, etc and went back to the ship in a bicycle taxi. Remember the three-wheeler bicycles the bakers have at home? They are similar to these taxis only these have an open box to sit in.

Incidentally, during the same afternoon we arrived at the Port of Batavia, or to give the native name – Tandjong Priok, we had an exciting half-hour when 27 of Nippon's aircraft flew over-head and dropped their bombs. As they were kept up to a great height by anti aircraft guns, the aim of the bombers was rotten and hardly any damage was done.

Next morning our ship went alongside a tanker to oil. Whilst oiling, a squadron of Nippon bombers escorted by fighters flew over the city and docks and after dropping their bombs a direct hit was scored on the oil-tanker but luckily the fire was quickly quenched.

On our starboard beam, three enemy fighters flew low over the oil-tanks and machine gunned the tanks causing two of them to burst into flame. The ship was soon black with smoke and the heat was intense.

At 1830 hrs we left Batavia for Surabaya and the following afternoon we dropped anchor in mid-stream.

It appears that Surabaya had a visit from Nippon's aircraft and the result was a burning oil tanker half sunk by the docks.

We oiled straight away and later that evening we received a message to the effect that aerial reconnaissance planes had sighted an enemy convoy proceeding towards Batavia. Half an hour later the Allied fleet comprising of the De Ruyter, Exeter, Houston, Java and Perth departed, preceded by ten destroyers.

All that night we sailed around looking for this convoy and it wasn't until 1600 hrs the following afternoon that we made contact.

Oh boy; did we make contact! Our force, numbering fifteen ships, was opposed by a Japanese Force of approximately thirty to forty ships. The battle raged on with ships on either side being sunk. It was four hours of relentless hell before both fleets retired to lick their wounds.

Our casualties were the De Ruyter, Java and Exeter sunk, Electra and four other destroyers sunk. The turrets of the Houston were out of action. Our damages, thank God, were negligible.

As far as I could ascertain, the losses of the Japanese Fleet were: three heavy cruisers, two light cruisers and several destroyers, not forgetting two submarines.

After the battle, the remainder of our Fleet made their way back to Batavia. When we arrived in our rather depleted force consisted of the Houston, an American destroyer, and Perth.

As we had to refuel and re-ammunition there wasn't any leave, and when extra life saving floats were brought on board, we never felt any happier. Gosh, I wished I was home with you.

> *We all realised that things were getting much tougher, and all of us were afraid for our future. I'd never seen so many big tough men turning to religion and praying.*

When the news circulated around that we could only get a third of the ammunition ordered, we felt very blue and to top it all news arrived of a Japanese convoy led by two cruisers approaching Batavia and about 80 miles away.

At 1900 hrs that fateful Saturday night, the Houston, Perth and an American destroyer left the wharves for a quick clean up of the Japanese convoy then to the south side of Java to pick up AIF troops, thence home to Fremantle. The idea was good, but things turned out rather different, as you will see in the next letter.

So I'll end this long letter by wishing you the best of everything,

Love
Fred xx

The last known photo of HMAS Perth in Tandjong Priok (Java), shows battle weary 'Perth' after day/night action in the Battle of Java Sea off the coast of Surabaya on the 27th February 1942

3rd March 1942

Dear Nola,

Here is the letter, as promised.

The night was nearly black, the stars were hidden by over-cast clouds and it suited us right down to the ground as we hoped to catch the enemy convoy by surprise.

We had left Batavia on 28-2-1942 with the crew at 1st degree of readiness, but at 2030 hrs, orders were piped for us to proceed to the 2nd degree of readiness.

The bugler sounded the 1st degree of readiness (Air Raid Yellow) followed by an announcement over the paging system. This meant that there were unidentified aircraft in the vicinity, and the duty watch manned the guns.

> *When the 2nd degree of readiness (Air Raid Red) was played and announced, everybody went to action stations.*

At approximately 2315 hrs, ships were seen on our starboard beam and immediately we received the wrong answer to our challenging light, so we opened fire.

The battle was on!

Instead of the enemy force consisting of two cruisers and several transports, we found out that the force consisted of 104 ships of which 45 were warships.

> *During the battle, Fred Lasslett was at the bottom of the ships bow where he was maintaining the gyro. (The Sperry Gyro was a compass that indicated true north based on rotation of the Earth around its axis.) This was a location where Fred could see the hull plates flex as depth charges exploded. As the battle intensified, he was ordered out of that dangerous location, and observed the remainder of the battle from the plotting room on the bridge.*

On and on went the battle and eventually it seemed that the Houston and Perth had a chance of passing through the Sunda Straits and to comparative safety.

Halfway through the Strait, the Captain noticed that the

Houston was lagging behind and in danger of being encircled, so we turned to cover her with our guns whilst she limped out.

Too late! The Japanese ships saw what we had done and made haste to encircle us, which they did.

The battle raged on faster and thicker, with Japanese ships going down left and right and the Houston and Perth by the Grace of God, still afloat.

Then, Bang! Like running into a brick wall, we stopped. We had been hit in the forward engine room by a torpedo.

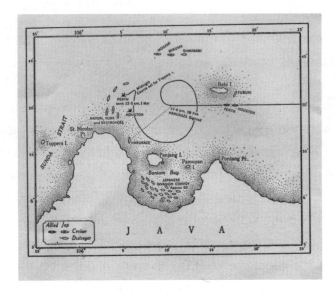

A minute later, "Abandon Ship" was piped and as the crew jumped, walked, ran or slid overboard, another torpedo hit us forward and the Japanese destroyers closed in on us, letting fly with every gun imaginable.

Whilst in the water, I found by somebody's watch that the battle had raged for one hour as the time was 0020 hrs.

With enemy ships zigzagging around the ocean, things weren't too healthy in the water, and, to add to our despondency we saw the Houston catch fire and sink about 20 minutes after we had been in the water.

We were drifting in the water with the survivors clinging to anything that would float.

The Japanese ships kept circling around, but they were only picking up their own survivors.

We stayed in that thick oily water for approximately ten hours, when much to our apprehension we were picked up by a Japanese boat. Imagine our relief when instead of shooting us, like we had been led to believe, they wiped the oil off us, clothed us and fed us. I reckon you could have heard the sigh of relief go up all around.

Whilst the Japanese destroyers were picking up the survivors, a Dutch plane flew overhead and naturally the destroyers and other ships increased speed and left the rest of the survivors in the water.

What happened to those boys, we don't know. Personally, I think they were eventually picked up by Japanese destroyers and taken to Surabaya.

Well Nola, later in the afternoon we were transferred to another destroyer and spent the night crowded together on the quarter-deck. To make matters worse, a drizzling rain started, so the crew threw a large piece of canvas over us. After a while the heat and stench of our oily bodies became so unbearable I decided to remain outside in the rain.

Late the following morning, we were transferred to the San Non Maru, a Japanese transport boat of approximately 5,000 tons and there we stayed for eight days.

Conditions on board weren't so bad. The ship was an old three decker and we were fortunate to be on the second deck.

Our food consisted of rice and fish; after being there for three days we were allowed to bring on supplies from an auxiliary yacht which was captured.

On board this ship were approximately 180 Perth boys and 120 Houston boys with a sprinkling of men from a mine-sweeper.

We were anchored within a hundred yards of the shore when word came around that we might go Shanghai and even Tokyo. When yours truly heard this I tried to get somebody to join me in an attempt to escape, but no luck.

Three times I tried to get others to escape with me, but no luck, and the day after the last attempt, we were transferred to the beautiful shores of Java.

It is there that I must leave you until the next letter, so until then, Au revoir,

Love Fred xx

<u>The following is a statement by the Minister for the Navy (The Honourable Norman J O Makin MP) in Parliament on 2nd March 1945.</u>

The Allied ships in the Java Sea Battle totalled two 8″ gun cruisers (HMS Exeter and USS Houston), one 6″ cruiser (HMAS Perth), two 5.9″ Dutch cruisers (HNMS De Ruyter and Java), and nine destroyers (HMS Electra, Encounter and Jupiter, USS John D. Edwards, John D. Ford, Alden and Paul Jones, and HNMS Kortenaer and Witte De With).

It has been estimated that the initial Japanese force comprised five cruisers and thirteen destroyers. One enemy 8-inch cruiser and one destroyer were probably sunk by gunfire and another 8-inch cruiser and a destroyer were damaged.

On the evening of 26th February, the Allied ships sailed from Surabaya under the command of Admiral Doorman, RNN, flying his flag in HNMS De Ruyter. Their objective was to intercept a Japanese convoy reported to be approaching north-eastern Java.

One of the USS Houston's gun turrets had already been put out of action by enemy air attack, but she sailed with the remainder of the force, and acquitted herself with distinction in the subsequent engagements with the enemy.

Enemy air attacks on the following morning were unsuccessful, and in the afternoon the Japanese cruisers and destroyers were sighted. The Allied forces at once increased speed to engage the enemy, and the 8-inch cruisers of both sides opened fire at 30,000 yards. The light cruisers and destroyers followed suit as soon as range permitted.

Perth's second salvo hit a Japanese destroyer and the enemy flotilla retired into a smoke screen. When the smoke cleared, one enemy destroyer was on fire, and she is thought to have sunk. At that stage too, Perth came under very heavy fire from the rearmost of the Japanese heavy cruisers.

About an hour later, HMS Exeter was damaged by an 8-inch shell, but was furnished with a smoke screen by Perth and destroyers. The Dutch destroyer Witte De With, screening Exeter, beat off a Japanese destroyer, scoring hits with two salvoes.

In the meantime HNMS Kortenaer was torpedoed amidship, broke in two and sank within a few minutes.

The flagship then led the cruisers in an attempt to get behind the enemy and attack his transports, and the Allied destroyers launched a counter-attack.

In bad visibility, HMS Electra probably scored hits with four salvoes on an enemy destroyer, but Electra herself was hit and stopped. Her guns were silenced one by one, and she sank about 6pm.

HMAS Perth, emerging through the smoke, was unsuccessfully attacked with torpedoes by enemy destroyers, and then joined issue with a Japanese 8-inch cruiser. The Australian ship's opening salvoes scored direct hits and subsequent salvoes also found their mark. When her target was last seen she was on fire and stationary, with her bows in the air. She probably sank.

Darkness had fallen when HMS Jupiter was torpedoed on the starboard side. She was immobilised by the attack, and sank about four hours later.

Throughout the night, enemy aircraft shadowed the Allied force, but shortly before midnight Perth had another success when she scored hits with at least two salvoes on an enemy cruiser.

At this stage double disaster met the Allies when HNMS De Ruyter (Flagship) and Java were lost – apparently as a result of torpedo attacks.

With the Allied cruiser strength reduced to his own ship and the damaged Houston, and knowing that the enemy still had at least four cruisers and twelve destroyers (besides the force, other than the initial one, which had entered the area) and a strong air reconnaissance, the Commanding Officer of Perth (Captain HML Waller, DSO, RAN) had no alternative but to order what remained of the striking force to withdraw.

HMS Encounter and the damaged Exeter succeeded in reaching Surabaya, as had the four American destroyers and the Dutch destroyer Witte De With. Exeter and Encounter sailed from there on the night of 28th February, enroute for Colombo, but the last message from them came next morning, when Exeter reported that she had sighted a force of enemy ships. Witte De With was bombed and sunk in Surabaya Harbour.

Meanwhile Perth and Houston threw off the enemy by a feint, and reached Tandjong Priok (Batavia) on the morning of 28th February.

After embarking fuel and additional fire-fighting equipment and rafts, as well as 4-inch ammunition, the two ships sailed together that night, to endeavour to pass through the confined waters of Sunda Straits during darkness, enroute for Tjilatjap. (On the south side of Java to embark 6th Army Division and return to Australia).

About 11:30pm – some three and a half hours after leaving Tandjong Priok – HMAS Perth signalled that she had sighted a destroyer near Sunda Strait. Later she amplified that signal to one cruiser.

That was the last message received from Perth or Houston. From that stage, the story is taken up by the four person- nel later rescued by US submarines after the sinking of a Japanese transport in the South China Sea.

It was after 11pm when one of Perth's lookouts reported a dark object on the starboard hand and a few minutes later the Australian cruiser's for'ard turrets opened fire.

> *The action lasted about one and a half hours. The numer- ical strength of the enemy is indicated by the fact that enemy gunfire came from several bearings, and that at some stages Japanese destroyers passed so close to the cruiser that they could be engaged with machine guns. Apart from making the maximum use of her gunfire, Perth was able to fire eight torpedoes during the action, four to port, and four to starboard. The exact effect of these could not be gauged, but next morning three enemy transports and one converted aircraft carrier were seen down by the stern and practically beached.*

Despite the overwhelming strength of the enemy, Perth was not hit until about 20 minutes after she opened fire. The first shell to strike her passed through her forward fun- nel and exploded, carrying away a sea-boat and doing considerable damage to the port pom-pom and flag deck.

Thereafter she suffered numerous hits, losing her aircraft and its catapult and crane, as well as the starboard pom-pom on the flag deck.

About that time, and with only ten minutes between them, two torpedoes struck the ship on the starboard side, the second in the forward engine room.

Some time later, a third torpedo hit was received – this time on the port side aft.

From the time of the first torpedoing, Perth was hit repeatedly by gunfire, from several bearings, and she finally sank at 35 minutes after midnight on the morning of the first of March.

USS Houston is reported to have sunk shortly afterwards.

The fate of Captain Waller is not known. He is reported to have been seen on the bridge, uninjured, after the second torpedo struck the ship. He gave the order: "Stand by to abandon ship"; and later: "Abandon ship; every man for himself".

HMAS Perth had a distinguished career in this war. She began her good work in the West Indies and carried on in the Middle East, where Allied soldiers from Greece and Crete knew and admired her fighting qualities.

Captain Waller and his men brought that heritage with them when they went into action in the Java Sea Battle and in the darkness of Sunda Straits. And it was a heritage that they did not betray. In both these actions they left their mark on the enemy, and their ship went down fighting against overwhelming odds.

A TRIBUTE TO THE

PERTH

We lost well high four hundred men
from the fairest land on the Earth.
They fought it out to the bitter end
And went down with the "Perth".

It was indeed a glorious action
Against over-whelming odds
And shows how Aussies stick it
When unfavoured by the Gods.

As the first guns thundered action
They were ready – undismayed
As the battle raged about them
Their courage was displayed.

For Steadfast to their duty
With Nelson as their guide
And comrades falling around them
Was thus they fought and died.

With all her shells expanded
She slid beneath the sea
And though her story's ended
Her name spells liberty.

So think o' them with honour
As they rest beneath the wave
They fought for King and Country
And sleep in sailor's grave.

SERANG

Dear Nola,

I landed on the shores of Java with the other survivors and after a short march we came onto eight motor trucks pulled up on the side of the road. In one of the trucks were men and women. I spoke to one of the women and found out that she was from Perth WA. I told her the number of prisoners from the Perth, as we thought that being a woman, she might be allowed to go free and perhaps get the news of survivors home. We climbed into the trucks and were driven to Serang, a town approximately 40 miles north of Batavia. We arrived at Serang in the afternoon and after a few delays we were locked up in the Bantam Park theatre.

That theatre was approximately 200 feet x 60 feet. The floor was tiled stone and the seats were removed. Sitting down back to back and not allowed to talk were roughly 600 prisoners including Dutch, Javanese and Indians.

Well Nola, you can imagine the discomfort and trials we had to endure. Our food consists of rice and a small amount of greens, potato leaves, I believe.

We arrived in the theatre on the 10th March. Things got so bad that nearly everybody had dysentery, about a dozen men still had shrapnel in their body, also a couple had fever and a few had malaria. Things got so bad that I made up my mind to escape and hide in a Dutchman's home in Batavia.

The Bantam Park Theatre in 1990.
Photo: N. Lasslett

I tried to get several persons to join me but no luck. So at 10.15 pm on Friday evening the 18th March, I made my way to the latrines which were in an alley way outside the theatre. I waited until the guard marched to the other end of the alley and then I jumped over the wall, over a roof, and then onto a kerosene tin roof of a house next door.

When I tested my weight on the roof it let out an awful squeak. I prayed to God that it would rain and believe it or not, out of a clear night came one of those sudden down-pours. Coincidence? Perhaps.

When the rain started I carefully edged my way down the shaky roof and with only a yard to go I felt a surge of relief come over me. But next step, Crash! Through the roof I went and landed on a number of bicycle taxis below.

My heart was in my mouth and I expected detection any moment, but my luck still held. After groping around in semi-darkness for a few minutes I found the door and coming out in the opening I came to a 7 ft fence. As I climbed the fence a small dog came out of the house barking loud enough to wake the dead. Needless to say, I wasted no time getting over that fence. I think I cleared that fence in the world record of three seconds.

From one yard to another I ran, hid and climbed until I came to a double gate leading onto a street. But as luck would have it, the gate was locked. I scouted around and found an iron bar and in half a minute I was free. A wave of exultation came over me, so down the street in full light I walked with head bowed so as to hide my face.

The rain was pouring down in torrents so I had the street to myself.

After walking for a hundred yards along this street I came to the main road and following instructions I had received from a Dutch air-force man, I stepped out for Batavia, roughly 40 miles away.

I walked and walked, passing through village after village, resting now and then, but with the thought of Batavia urging me on. Before I had left I had heard rumours that the AIF (Australian Imperial Force) were fighting on the outskirts of Batavia, but I was very doubtful. Now I had the chance to find out whether the rumour was true or not.

So on and on I went until five o'clock the following morning when I arrived at a fairly large village by the name of Palambang. At this village, the bridge over a wide, swiftly flowing river was wrecked, and as the river was too hard to swim over in my weakened condition and dawn was near, I crept alongside the river and hid among the coconut and banana trees.

Well my love, I'll have to continue the story in the next letter so until then, Au revoir,

Love Fred xx

Dear Nola,

Here I am again – now to continue the story.

I hid among the trees until well into the morning. About 200 yards from where I was hiding were a few native houses with no sign of movement from them.

Being by this time hungry and thirsty, I approached the houses, but as I got near I could hear the sound of children, so I stole back to my hiding place. With about ten yards of open ground to clear I heard a shout from behind, and turning around I noticed a native boy gesticulating at me. Needless to say, I went for my life amidst the trees, and before long I could hear several persons in full chase. Boy-o-boy did I make speed.

Ten minutes later the sound of the huntsmen grew fainter and fainter, and yours truly again went into hiding, feeling as weak as a kitten.

By now, the sun was well over-head and I was feeling the pangs of hunger and thirst, so taking a chance I prowled around to find a stick long enough to reach the coconuts. After a while I found one and after several attempts I finally dislodged a coconut. The next problem was to remove the tough husk and as I never had a knife, I tried with my bare hands, needless to say I failed. In desperation I made up my mind to accost a native digging up the soil 50 yards away.

When I walked towards him I was afraid that he would up and away, but as I drew near him I noticed that he had a large native knife in his hand. It was my turn to grow afraid, but with the pangs of hunger in my mind I overcame my fear.

When I was in speaking distance, I made signs to show that I was friendly and also hungry, so it was with a glad heart, that when he sliced the top off the coconut, he handed it back to me to drink. After I had satisfied my thirst, he split the coconut in four and I satisfied my hunger. Then and there, that humble coconut tasted like the sweetest thing on earth.

I again went into hiding, keeping an eye on the native and ten minutes later, he arose and ambled out of sight. I was in doubt as to whether he had gone for a bag of seeds or something similar, or to tell his friends that he had seen a foreign white devil or whatever they suppose to call us. I wasn't in doubt for long, for over the hill came a crowd of roughly thirty natives, so with thoughts of being captured and perhaps beheaded, I left the vicinity in double quick time. Again into hiding I went, this time a few miles from my captors.

Thirty minutes went by and I was thinking that I had given them the slip, when I heard the sound of many voices. Closer and closer came the voices, and when through the leaves of the bushes I was hiding in, I could see the natives, I nearly stopped breathing in case they heard me. They looked here, searched there and to my taut nerves it seemed that they knew I was here, but they wanted to play around like a cat plays with a mouse.

The suspense became unbearable and I wanted to scream out aloud. And when a knife missed me by a foot, I nearly did, but it was a native clearing away through the dense under-growth. Three of the natives stopped to have a confab about three feet away and I did stop breathing for a while.

After the confab, the natives again started to search and I knew it was only a matter of time, so when I heard a voice calling the natives, I knew I was captured. I was quite calm and resigned when they ordered me out.

Well my love, I think that will do until the next letter, so until then, again I say Au revoir,

Love Fred xxx

Dear Nola,

Once again I start my weekly letter.

Last week's letter ended where I was captured, so I'll continue from there.

Out into the ring of gesticulating natives I crawled, and when I rose to my feet I was confronted by a crowd of roughly 40 to 50 men, women and children. Imagine my relief, when instead of a native rushing at me with a knife, one of them offered me a coconut which I gladly accepted.

After I drank the milk and ate portion of the coconut, the procession started across the paddy fields towards the village with the proud and haughty prisoner in the lead. Or something like that.

During the walk I asked the leader as to whether he was going to hand me over to the Japanese and with many signs and the little English he knew, he told me that he and his friends hated the Japs and were going to hide me.

I cheered up at this news; although I was very suspicious. When we eventually reached the village and stopped before a private house I nearly believed them.

Out of the house came an old woman, and after speaking to the leader of our large procession, we marched on again.

When we came to the main street, I was offered cigarettes and rice cakes and other food which I thoroughly enjoyed.

Down the street we marched, with the native men, women and kids yelling like mad, until at the end of the street I came to the police station. When I saw the Japanese flags flying and the native police with the Jap arm bands on I wasn't very surprised. I turned to the leader and pointed to the flags and policemen but he made a motion of pulling off the arm bands and then pointing a finger to his head, making out, that if they never wore the arm bands or flew the flags, the Japanese would shoot them. At the same time he was saying, "Japanese no good" and running his finger across his throat.

Once again my hopes rose and when they gave me more food, pots of tea and then allowed me to walk around the back to wash the mud off my body, I was beginning to doubt my eyes.

Just then I heard a bell ringing and a large crowd gathered before the police station and the leader stood on a box and argued with the people, so it seemed.

I had a fair idea that I would know my fate in the next ten minutes, so it was with a queer feeling in my throat that I awaited the outcome of his speech.

Well my love, I'll have to postpone the rest of the story until next week, so once again I say Au revoir,

Love Fred xx

Dear Nola,

With your ever-fresh memory before me I sit down to continue this story.

I sat waiting for the leader to find out what the crowd wanted, and it was with a feeling of uneasiness that I noticed he had finished addressing the crowd and was walking towards me. He appeared to be in doubt and when he told me that he was going to hide me at his place, which was situated a few miles along the road, I once again became cheerful. So later that day, 2.30pm I think, three of us climbed into a gharry and off we went.

The ride was exhilarating. Every now and then we passed Japanese soldiers in motor cars and on bicycles, and because the gharry was an open type I was in plain view the whole time. However, my luck still held and we weren't stopped.

We had travelled several miles along flat country at a fairly decent speed, but when the country changed from flat to slightly hilly country, the horse refused to pull the load. Much to my disgust, the driver climbed out of the gharry and belted the horse with a whip. Being their prisoner and not wanting to attract attention I could only sit and watch but I made a vow that if I ever came across that fellow in other circumstances, it would be another story. I would belt him the same way he'd beaten the horse.

This went on for close on half an hour and at one point two Japanese soldiers on bicycles, slowed up and nearly turned back. Needless to say, it never improved my likening for the driver. The other two passengers never said anything, so it seemed to me that these incidents were everyday affairs.

At 3.30pm we came to a village and with a crowd of natives we stopped before a large house which later I found to be the Residence house. In here we went and were confronted by a large, fat Javanese. The guard handed over a sheaf of papers and after perusing them he asked my name, nationality and service. After dismissing me, I was fed again and a little while later I was back in another gharry with my two captors.

On the journey, I asked them where we were going and was told, back to the police station. After a while we came to the outskirts of a town and I had the feeling that I had been here before so when the Hotel Vos loomed up in sight I knew I was lost. Up to the Hotel, which was the head-quarters of Nippon, we merrily rode, and up for more questions I went. The same questions were asked and the same answers were given and after a while I hoped that I would be taken to the local gaol and the news of my escape and capture kept hidden. Into the gharry climbed my two captors, but this time minus little Freddie, for I was marched away by two guards. Along the streets we marched, turning here turning there until in the distance loomed the Cinema Theatre.

When we marched to the doorway, out rushed half a dozen Japanese yelling at the top of their voices and brandishing their rifles.

Well my elusive girl, I'll have to continue my story in my next letter so until then I'll say Au revoir,

Love Fred xxx

Dear Nola,

Today is the first month anniversary of our tragic fight and looking back it was a month of hectic activity.

But, to continue my story.

Out of the theatre rushed a crowd of Japanese soldiers, including one Japanese who was a Sergeant. In his hands he held a piece of paper and on it I noticed my name, rank and age. He asked me if I was the person whose name was on the paper. Taking a chance, I decided to bluff them out, so I said the name on the paper was my brother's and that I had been hiding in the hills. At this announcement they flew into a babble of talk and after a few minutes argument they marched me inside.

I was marched into a small room and ordered to sit down. Standing around me were five Officers with not exactly the kindest of expressions on their face. Also in the room was a Dutchman who interpreted for the Japanese. Then the ordeal began.

Once again I was asked whether I had escaped from here, and once again I told them that it was my brother. This went on for twenty minutes or so, and as they seemed to be in doubt my spirits once again started to rise. At this point an officer sent one of the guards into the theatre and a few minutes later he came back with a fellow ship-mate by the name of Wray. The Officer asked Wray whether I was "who I am" and although I shouted to Wray that I was Fred Lasslett's brother, it was too late. Away went Wray and his guard and in the small room there was intense silence for a moment, then the Officers found their voices.

"Liar!" they cried. "You tell untruths", and with that they unsheathed their swords and poor little Freddie expected his head to roll off any minute.

After five minutes of suspense and abuse, the Jap sergeant bashed me. Two of the Japanese Army officers ordered me to show them how I escaped. This I did.

The boys in the hall told me later, that since the Japanese had taken the count this morning and found that I was missing, they had threatened all sorts of dire ends if I wasn't recaptured. So when I walked in surrounded by Japanese officers, they sighed with relief, then pity, for they thought I was going to be beheaded in the alley-way.

After showing them how I had escaped, I was marched back to the room and beaten several times. I was then handed over to three guards. Before I was marched away, the officer gave one of the guards his automatic revolver and showed him how to release the safety catch.

Down the streets we marched and thinking this was my last walk I seemed to notice things which ordinarily I would not have. Although the place was filthy, and the people dirty, and most of the world was at war with each other, life at that moment was the most desired thing in my life. I thought, what a stupid way to die.

We eventually arrived at the local native gaol and when they placed me against a brick wall and the guards lined up like a firing party I knew I was finished.

People say that during the last moments of a person's life, flashes of their past deeds and misdeeds appear before their eyes. Well, personally speaking, my mind was a blank.

I couldn't think of a single thing.

My only thought was what a lovely day it was.

The two guards raised their rifles to shoot me, but for some unknown reason the sergeant stopped the count. One of them took me by the arm, pushed me into a solitary cell, and locking the door, left me.

I don't know why they did not shoot me. But I found out later that the Japanese respect bravery, and I had shown no sign of being afraid. However, they also believe that a crazy man should not be harmed in any way - until the evil spirits have left his body. I prefer to believe that I fall into the first category.

I was in a cell approximately 8 feet x 4 feet composed of concrete floor, walls and ceiling. Outside this cell was a small courtyard with a rectangular brick water container called a mandi, for bathing.

Imagine my surprise when on the following day in walked a crowd of Dutch and Javanese women with the intentions of bathing at the mandi. They did this by getting the water from the mandi with a tin container. When they saw me they were momentarily confused, but as luck would have it, there was a wooden outer door as well as a steel door on my cell. After they had finished their bathing, they went out and later returned with bread and fruit. This went on for four days, so I never minded the solitary confinement.

One Eurasian girl who was very kind to me was a girl whose name was Naida. She used to risk the displeasure of the guards by sneaking over to my cell and cheering me up with a few English words she could pronounce. By this time I had a slight attack of dysentery which was rife at the Cinema and I was feeling very blue, so I prayed to God to get me out of this cell. That was in the afternoon of March the 23rd, Wednesday to be exact.

Later that afternoon four American sailors were brought into the prison. Three of them were locked up in the cell next to mine, and the fourth, Commander Epstein, an American doctor, was locked up in mine. The following morning the five of us were paraded before a Japanese Sergeant and an American doctor by the name of Burroughs, and our names and sickness, if any, were written down.

Serang Gaol Well, Java

The four Americans were locked in another cell (K5) and I was locked up in (K6) cell, a cell used for dysentery prisoners. In this cell were 30 other American and Australian prisoners and once again I was with some of my shipmates.

While there, an American who was dying told his mates to knock out his gold fillings after he died, so that they could buy additional food, which they did.

The following morning I was marched to the Office and once again I gave my name, age and rank. When I told the Sergeant my rank, a Javanese man, who I later found to be the head gaol keeper, wanted to know whether I could fix the lights in the gaol, this I did and that's how I became gaol electrician. For the remainder of the week I repaired the lights and fuses in the gaol with the assistance of an Australian, Goldie by name, and an American, Burgoine. The post of gaol electrician was a godsend, as it enabled me to be out in the sun most of the day, instead of being cramped up in a cell built for fifteen natives, but housing 30 to 40 of us.

In one cell built for ten natives measuring 10 feet x 8 feet were locked 26 persons and to make matters worse, the wooden door had a window of roughly 9" square. They were so crowded that they couldn't lie down to sleep and had to save the barrelled water by having a wash every alternate day.

Added to this was that the people suffering with dysentery had a small bucket about 2 feet high for their use. With this and the stench off their bodies, the place was unbearable.

The following week I was allowed to go outside the gaol on my own and to the local market with a guard.

This went on for a couple of weeks and there was great excitement when the boys built bakery ovens and later baked bread.

On Monday 13th April, we got orders to pack our scanty belongings as we were on our way to Batavia, and late that morning we climbed into trucks and off we went to Batavia arriving at the Batavia Bicycle Camp barracks, late in the afternoon.

The conditions in these barracks after our Serang ordeal were as different as chalk and cheese and when we found that the barracks were already occupied by the AIF prisoners, we were on the look out for friends. Imagine our delight when we heard that the meals consist of bread and meat and vegetable stews.

Well my love, I'll leave you here and continue the story in the next letter, so once again Au revoir,

Love Fred xx

DEEP THOUGHTS
PVTE L.V. WILLEY

Bicycle Camp Batavia 1942

1)

The boy sitting on the cot
Was in a melancholy mood.
He wasn't thinking of folks at home
Or cutting down of food.
He just had something on his mind
That was causing him despair.
And kept mumbling to himself,
'I know, it isn't fair.'
He got up and kicked a stone
Then stared off into space,
Still struggling with the problem
He knew that he must face.

2)
Half an hour later
When someone cut him down
They read his suicidal note
With quite a puzzled frown;
"Dear Dad and Mum", it ran
I've been through quite a lot,
And I've never once complained
Since the day that I was caught
I've fought bombers, cruisers, submarines
Anything that came along,
And carried out my orders,
Whether they were right or wrong.

3)
But tonight something happened,
That is causing all this grief
I could not quite believe my eyes,
It was tragically beyond belief.
Man's inhumanity to man,
Has once more been proven again
And if my death will right this wrong
I will not have died in vain
This has happened three times before
So please don't grieve for me
I waited all day for evening coffee,
And darned if it wasn't tea.

THE BICYCLE CAMP

Instructions

The Nippon Government has now formally established the Java Prisoner's Camp and appointed Officers to take charge of the prisoners.

The regular work for me to do is to supervise all the prisoners in the camp.

Therefore, everybody should observe every order of the Chiefs and Officers in order to perform your duties according to the ordinances of the Nippon Army and must keep in mind that you shall not impair the honour of your country.

I am hoping to meet you later, shall at present send this message, just mentioning what I wish, as I have been appointed to the post.

Masatoshi Sainto
Major General,
Chief of the Java Prisoner's camp.
Batavia, August 20th, the 17th year of Syoona.

2nd May 1942

Dear Nola,

Whilst we were in Serang we had heard all sorts of rumours, including the rumour that Italy had capitulated, and that England had invaded France, not mentioning that there was fierce fighting at Bandeong and Surabaya. When we arrived at Batavia, we heard the truth; things were practically the same as when we were captured. Adding of course, the capture of Java.

The second day in the new camp I met a few AIF soldiers from my home town. They happened to see the fight from where they were on the coast, and after hearing their version of the battle and my own idea of how the fight finished, I think the Japanese boats sunk or damaged consisted of three heavy cruisers, five cruisers, eight destroyers and two transports, and a converted aircraft carrier. Half of these ships were either sunk or damaged by their own side. The Japanese were under the impression that there were more than two ships against them, so in the darkness and confusion, they mistakenly fired torpedoes at their own ships.

As time went by, we firmly settled down to camp routine, for although we were Japanese prisoners, we were under our own Officers and NCOs. On the 20th May, I was made Camp Electrician.

> *Life in the camp was fairly monotonous for the POW's,*
> *So it was decided to put the case to the Japanese for pro-*
> *ducing concerts. The argument that it would relieve the*
> *boredom of the POW's and entertain the Japanese was*
> *accepted.*

During the following days plans were made to organise a concert for the men.

Naturally, I did the wiring of the lights and after much scrounging around, I managed to gather enough fittings and wire to illuminate the stage with seven 40 watt globes.

> *We even had a one foot by three foot sign which read*
> *"Fred Lasslett - Illumination Director".*

Along came Saturday night the 26th and before a crowded hall, a vaudeville type of concert was put on. Needless to say the show was a huge success and it augured well for forthcoming shows. The producer of the shows was Norm Carter of radio fame, but as the shows went on, an American soldier, Tex McFarland, produced a show.

About this time the Camp Commandant Susuki thought that the camp discipline needed strengthening, so he gave orders for the Japanese guards to knock it into us – which they did. The guards bashed everybody they could see.

But apart from the trials and tribulations, the camp could have been much worse. We had plenty of space to organise sport and it wasn't long before many games were being played. A volleyball tournament was arranged between the huts, and after many exciting games, the grand final went to the American Artillery in Hut I.

Well my love once again I must leave you, Au revoir,

Love Fred xx

Bicycle Camp Batavia 1942

JAPANESE ORDER OF THE DAY

10 - 7 - 1942

REPLY HONESTLY ABOUT WHAT THE JAPANESE FORCE ASK YOU.

IF YOU ANSWER INCORRECT, YOU WILL BE PUNISHED SEVERELY.

EXAMPLE:

1)   IF YOU KNOW THAT A CERTAIN PART OF AUSTRALIA, CANNOT BE PASSED BY MOTOR OR ON FOOT, ON ACCOUNT OF FOREST OR MARSH, AND YOU ANSWER THAT IT CAN BE PASSED, WE GO TO THE PLACE AND SUFFER HARDSHIPS, BELIEVING YOUR ANSWER.

2)   IN SPITE OF KNOWING THERE IS TRAFFIC ORGANIZATION. BELIEVING YOUR ANSWER, THERE IS NONE, WE FIND TRAFFIC ORGANIZATION IN YOUR DISTRICT.

BUT FOR THE LYING PROPAGANDA OF THE SENIOR MEN OF YOUR COUNTRY, YOU WOULD NOT HAVE MET WITH THE HARDSHIPS AS PRISONERS-OF-WAR.

BECAUSE YOU BELIEVED THEM:

YOU CAME HERE TO FIGHT US.

YOU SURRENDERED.

YOU ARE PRISONERS-OF-WAR.

I AM SORRY FOR THIS.

DIA-NIPPON IS A JUST COUNTRY AND DOES NOT USE LYING PROPAGANDA, SO DO EVERYTHING HONESTLY AND BE WELL REPAID.

**BY COMMANDANT
SUSUKI**

Bicycle Camp, Batavia

7th August 1942

Dear Nola,

As you will notice by the above date I have skipped six or more weeks, but as nothing startling happened during that period, I didn't want to bore you, so I'll commence the letter regarding what happened this month.

Previously we had signed a paper saying we would obey the Japanese officers and soldiers as long as the orders were not opposed to our oath to our King. So when another paper came around for us to sign saying that we would do anything Dia Nippon Sun ordered, we decided not to sign it.

Much to our dismay we were marched to the Japanese office, and with Japanese guards on either side we were forced to sign the paper. A few of our officers and men refused to sign, but after a belting they changed their mind.

As a punishment, the concert, canteen and other privileges were stopped. Also we had to stay in our compounds. A week later our privileges were granted and on July 23rd the concert was reopened. By this time the concert had grown to a cast of approximately 60 actors, and I had wired the theatre with 33 lights.

Instead of a vaudeville type of program we were presenting plays and musical comedies. We had Frank Purtell, late of JC Williams, to do the costume part of it, and a wig maker from Victoria, to make the girls wigs which he made out of sand bags.

On July 29th a Japanese command performance was given. The performance was from 8 o'clock until 10.30. As a mark of their gratitude, we were presented with a box of cigars and also a piano.

From then on, things settled down to the old routines, with face slapping and beatings included.

Later in the week the building of a bakery commenced and in thirteen days they were producing bread. The daily issue consisted of a 1/2 lb loaf of bread.

Well my love, nothing else startling happened for quite a while so at this point I'll end the letter by wishing you the best of everything.

Love Fred xx

14th August 1942

Dear Nola,

Once again I continue these letters.

At present I'm balancing this book on a tin box I found, so excuse the scribbling.

This week we were issued with tinned sausages and a Dutch dish of Nassi-gorrem, a dish comprising of fried rice and meat and vegetables. The rumour went around that owing to the shortage of rice, the Japanese were going to feed us on tinned stuff.

Needless to say we were elated, but not for long, for day after day we were fed on the usual rice and stew.

We were told that further medical supplies could not be

guaranteed by the Japanese, and as there were a considerable number of sick persons in the hospital and camp, things weren't too good.

Another rumour going around was that we were going to be paid in the near future. Apart from that, life went on in the usual routine so the next letter I'll write will start from Oct 1st so until then, again I say Au revoir,

Love Fred xx

JAPANESE A.R.P. ORDERS AND SIGNALS

(15 - 8 - 1942)   LIGHTS ON VERANDAHS AND LATRINES TO BE EXTINGUISHED UNTIL FURTHER ORDERS

2)   LIGHTS IN BARRACK ROOMS TO BE BROWN – OUT EFFECTIVELY

3)   NO SMOKING ON VERANDAH OR OUTSIDE AFTER DARK.

(A)		SIREN	OSCILLATION OF LIGHTS	BELL
	DANGER YELLOW	1.30 SEC, BLAST	10 SEC,	10 STROKES
	DANGER	1.20 SEC,	2 (2 SEC,)	—
(B)				
	ATTACK RED	20 SEC, BLAST	5 (2 SEC,)	
	ATTACK-PASSED WHITE	1.30 SEC, BLAST	1 (10SEC)	

IT WILL BE NOTICED THAT THE ATTACK SIGNAL AND THE ATTACK PASSED SIGNAL ARE SIMILAR, BUT WHEN THE SIGNAL IS USED AFTER ATTACK, IT SIGNIFIES AS STATED, ATTACK PASSED.

> *As the camp electrician, I was allowed to pass between the various compounds, accompanied by a guard. This allowed me to pass news from a secret wireless throughout the camp.*

8th October 1942

Dear Nola,

To continue. Things in general were much the same, and the only excitement was the rumour that we would get paid. A few days later I was paid the princely sum of 30 cents for my work as the official camp electrician. The rate of pay was 25 cents for Officers, 20 cents for W/Officers, 15 cents for Sergeants and 10 cents for Privates.

Well Nola, Japanese plans were going into action and on Sunday the 5th October, 1500 prisoners were ordered to get Anti-Tetanus, Dysentery and Cholera needles and be prepared to leave the camp three days later.

All day Wednesday the different troops were sorted out and their luggage searched. During the early hours of the following morning they marched out for a destination unknown. Later we heard that they had proceeded to Bangkok, Capital of Siam.

We that were left were ordered to change from our respective huts to hut 4 and hut 5, and after getting settled, imagine our chagrin when another list of names were announced on the following day. Once again my name and approximately 20 others weren't announced and it appeared that we were going to be left behind so as to keep the camp neat and orderly.

Then, whilst at dinner I was ordered to report at the Orderly Office, and on arriving I and twenty other persons were told to prepare to leave at 6 o'clock in the evening. After a few enquiries, I found that the lot of us were technicians, and that the main crowd were leaving in the morning. During the afternoon we marched down to the Japanese Office and there met approximately 88 American technicians. After having our luggage searched we were told that we were going to a cold place, which we guessed to be Japan.

After we had been issued with warm clothing and overcoats, lent by the remainder of the crowd who were told that they were going to a warm climate, we had an early tea. After saying good-bye to our friends we left the camp at 6.30pm in motor trucks.

Well my elusive girl I'll continue in the next letter.

Love Fred xx

To Changi and Japan

Dear Nola,

Once again I'll continue the story.

We were only in the trucks approximately 20 minutes, when we disembarked at the RAF prison at Glodok. There we marched out accompanied by Englishmen, Dutch and Eurasians. After 20 minutes walk we arrived at the railway station and after approximately 25 minutes travelling we landed at Tandjong Priok, the Port of Batavia.

Disembarking, we had another 45 minutes walk, and eventually reached another prison camp. We spent the night there, and early the following morning we marched to the docks.

Imagine our surprise when we once again met our mates we had left in the Bicycle Camp.

Very shortly, the whole crowd of us were transferred by barges to a 5,000 ton merchant ship which we found to be the Dai Nichi Maru. When everybody was on board the anchor was raised and our voyage started. Life on board was miserable as we were crowded like cattle, the food was only fair and there were no such things as toilet arrangements.

Four days later we anchored off Singapore, and the following morning we landed. Ashore we climbed into motor trucks and proceeded to the prison barracks at Changi. Half an hour later we were in the barracks with the technicians in one building and the rest in another. There conditions were quite good, and our food consisted of stew and rice plus Red Cross supplies, which also included heavy South African boots.

We stayed at Changi for eleven days and on the 26th October we embarked on trucks for the docks again. During the afternoon we went on board a 12,000 ton merchant ship which was converted into a semi-hospital ship. On board this ship we were immersed in lime water and our clothes fumigated. After the debugging we dressed and after a wait of two hours we walked aboard the Tojuku Maru, a vessel of approximately 5,000 tons.

Whilst in Singapore I was impressed by the beauty of the surrounding country. The foliage is vivid green with a freshness of its own. There are well made roads and the country in general is comprised of undulating hills and small scintillating lakes. The harbour consists of thousands of tiny inlets and surrounding Singapore proper are several islands large and small. The town itself is nothing startling, although there are some fine buildings and well made thoroughfares.

To continue: We boarded the Tojuku Maru on Monday 26th and the following morning we sailed for Saigon.

Conditions on board the ship were worse than the Dai Nichi Maru and it wasn't long before the troops were dying. We were crowded below deck, and many were suffering from dysentery, malaria and other sicknesses. The stench of infected wounds and disease was overpowering. The toilets were makeshift boxes assembled over the edge of the ship.

There were approximately 1200 prisoners and 600 Japanese soldiers on board, so when the Japs called for people who could cook, I quickly volunteered and got a job in the cook-house. The food was not only terrible but very light, so it wasn't long before the prisoners were down with dysentery, and the healthy ones were exchanging watches and clothing for food.

> *Many other Japanese ships carrying POW's were thought to be troopships and were sunk by the allies. However, the Tojuku Maru was slow and stayed close to the coast, and thus avoided attention from the Allies.*

On Wednesday 4th November, we dropped anchor at the mouth of the river leading to Saigon, seventeen miles up river, and the following morning we proceeded twelve miles up river to take on supplies and repair steam pipes.

We were there three days and on the 8th November, we set sail for Japan. After a nightmarish voyage, we arrived at the port of Moji. The total number of deaths on the voyage from Singapore to Moji was 27. We disembarked at Moji, which consists of a town hewn out of the mountains, with the houses stacked tightly together.

Once ashore our luggage was again searched. This was on Friday 27th November. After the search we were marched to a building where we were fed on rice, fish and raw vegetables. At 11.30 pm, we marched to the railway station and boarded a train which pulled out at 12.22 am.

For three days and two nights we ate and slept in trains. After passing through Kobe and Tokyo which are both intensely industrified, we eventually arrived at Karmachi and then by train to Ohasi, our eventual destination. We arrived on Monday 30th November, and were settled in a new barrack building with eight men to a room. Conditions are pretty good, although the food is only fair.

Well Nola, my elusive girl, as time is short I'll continue these letters at a later date. So until then, Au revoir,

Love Fred xx

OHASI

1st December 1942

Dear Nola,

As I explained in my previous letter, conditions are fairly good and the first part of the night I dreamt and wondered how you were. The weather here is very cold and usually snows at evening time. About 40% of us are sick, with either colds or dysentery. Today being Monday the 1st, it seems years since the Perth was sunk, instead of nine months.

By this time, with not much news of the progress of the war, the POWs had to accept that they could be imprisoned for many years. All that could be done was to make the best of the situation.

Tuesday night was bath night and did we need it. The water was steaming hot and I enjoyed the bath immensely. It was my first bath in nine months. The bath was a large wooden tub in the village bath-house. We were separated from the local women in the adjoining room by a timber wall with paper frames.

On Friday a Dutchman died of dysentery and was cremated on Sunday. I assisted in carrying the body. We held a small service in English.

Sunday afternoon we had 30 minute physical drill.

Well my love that is a rather concise letter of what happened during our first week at our new camp so until further news I'll say Au revoir,

Love Fred xx

7th December 1942

Dear Nola,

I wonder if you can imagine where I am and what I'm doing at the present moment.

This week gone by was full of incidents. Monday, four of my fellow prisoners died from dysentery or colds. The rest of us had to climb two miles up a mountain path to collect firewood for the cremation of the bodies.

The following day we carried the bodies to the crematorium. I marched in front with a paper wreath and on arriving, a funeral ritual was performed and then back we went. The following day the ashes were buried in the cemetery and a funeral service followed with the Japanese represented by the Camp Commandant and several other Japanese soldiers.

When I first experienced war and people died around me, it was fairly traumatic. But as time goes on, you steel your mind against feeling for the dead. They may have been good blokes, but I feel fortunate that it wasn't me.

The rest of the week was taken up with exercises and mountain walks. Friday night we had a hot bath. Sunday afternoon a party of us went to work at the mine, carrying both loose bricks and mud. The work isn't strenuous but it is very cold. The meals usually consist of rice-barley and fish or vegetables and are pretty fair.

Well my love, that comprises the news for the time being so until next week Au revoir,

Love Fred xxx

14th December 1942

Dear Nola,

Once again I write this letter to that elusive person back home, and as I write, I wonder what you would be doing now.

This week we worked on the rock pile on the hill and Wednesday our routine was altered by visitors of the Nippon Government. The following days we worked by a school house, making a path leading to a Memorial Shrine which was unveiled on Sunday.

Saturday night, two American sailors and one Dutch soldier died of pneumonia and Sunday a party of us marched to the Cemetery, dug the graves and later in the afternoon we buried the bodies.

Well my love, that finishes the news for the time being, so until further along the road of time I say Au revoir,

Love Fred xxx

-: The Oath :-

I make an oath that I obey all orders of Dia Nippon Military Men and do not make light of escape resistance or disobedient manner.

I make an oath in works that I act strictly by rules of Dia Nippon Sun and never oppose all orders of Dia Nippon Military Men and of Clerks in charge of works.

I make an oath that if I make an opposite action against above two oaths I receive any severe punishments willingly by The Nippon Sun Law.

I swear above Three Oaths

No. 103
Name F.W. Lasslett

Aerial view of Ohasi POW Camp
Photograph by Hiroe Iwashita

21st December 1942

Dear Nola,

I suppose back home everybody is in the midst of shopping fever and although there is a war I'm sure that this Christmas will be as merry as others gone by.

In Japan the weather is typical English Xmas weather, fine sunny mornings and snow during the afternoons and evenings.

The work we are doing is general navvy work. The hours are usually 8am - 11.30am then 1.00pm - 4.30pm seven days a week.

On Christmas Day we didn't work, and one hour during the morning and night, we had religious services.

Boxing Day we worked, and so settled down to our daily routine.

Well my love, that finishes the news for the time being so until further news, I'll say Au revoir,

Love Fred xx

28th December 1942

Dear Nola,

Once again I start a weekly letter hoping that you won't be bored by the contents.

Work went on as usual with the days becoming cold and colder, the average temperature varied between 34° Fahrenheit to 20° below freezing. Well, when you are working out in the open, especially shifting plate-iron, the work isn't exactly congenial.

This week we had a few more inspections by important Nippons.

New Years Eve we celebrated by a sing song during the evening, but as I was tired I never welcomed in the New Year.

New Years Day started with an increase of rice and also a holiday. There was much rejoicing and drinking of Sake in the village. We drank water.

Well my love as it is time to go to bed, I'll continue this letter at a later date.

Love Fred xxx

4th January 1943

Dear Nola,

With thoughts of you foremost in my mind I continue these weekly letters.

This week was rather different from the others. On Tuesday I had a fight with an American – the result was a draw. The American was caught stealing food from another POW, so I hit him.

Wednesday we were visited by Colonel Hakatiyama, Commander of Prison Camps in this area. He is a short, plump, elderly person. After the inspection we expected a cigarette issue but alas, in vain.

Thursday I was elected room Chief. The rest of the week was as usual.

> *The role of room chief was really to keep the peace. This meant controlling the moods of the men so that they did not fight amongst themelves, or upset the guards.*

Well my love, that is all for the week so until further news, Au revoir,

Love Fred xx

Fred Lasslett's
War Diaries - part 2

The following letters, for the period 11-1-43 to 3-7-44, were written by Fred Laslett, in pencil, onto cigarette paper sheets, which were concealed from the Japanese.

11th January 1943

Dear Nola,

All this week I have been working on the foundations of the new guard-house at our new camp.

The place which I am levelling off was originally a potato and radish patch, and it is only the hope of coming across one of those vegetables that keeps a person digging. The ground is frozen because the weather is usually around 12–15° below freezing point.

Monday morning, Colonel Hakatiyama visited the camp. The same night we had a cigarette and soap issue.

Wednesday we were told to leave two of the stoves out during the day & night except for certain hours. Friday we had another cigarette issue.

Saturday I didn't work, so I did my washing. Sunday I worked down at the other camp.

During the week we were told that some time in the future we would go to work at our respective trades, so we are all looking forward to the time when we will be working at our old trades again. Well love, once again I say Au revoir,

Love Fred xxx

18th January 1943

Dear Nola,

Once again I pen a few lines so as to let you know how I am keeping.

Monday I went to work at the new camp. The weather is still cold, 12–15° below freezing.

Tuesday the weather was slightly warmer.

On Wednesday we had a change of guards. The guards gave us cigarettes as a parting gift. They belonged to the 62nd Garrison; the new guards belong to the 64th Garrison and have never been anywhere else on duty. So far they seem to be a decent crowd, so we are hoping for the best.

Thursday we were told that in future we would work ten days and have one holiday. Needless to say it is rather tough to wash and dry clothes.

Friday I tasted my first piece of fish meat for eight weeks and that was a few small pieces in the stew.

The main topic of conversation is either about food or Armistice.

Saturday night was bath night. That means approximately 30–40 persons trying to bathe in a tub about 4' x 3'. Needless to say it is a bit of a squeeze.

Well my love, that finishes the news for the time being so until next week I say Au revoir.

Love Fred xx

PS: As there is only one hour difference in time between the two countries, I'm always imagining what you would be doing.

Prisoners of war in a POW camp near Ohasi, Japan. The prisoners include a dozen men from the USS Houston, several Americans from the 131st Field Artillery, and Australians from the Australian Imperial Forces and the HMAS Perth. Gift of Henry Thew.

31st January 1943

Dear Nola,

Like the ever-returning bad penny, here I am again.

Life out here is pretty well the same. We still go to work at our new camp where the ground is frozen hard and the temp is still around 14–20° Fahrenheit.

The usual routine is to start our 1 1/2 mile walk at 8 o'clock and arrive at the job at 8.30am. We would work until 11 o'clock then go back for lunch. After lunch we proceed back to work at 1 o'clock and finish at 4 o'clock.

According to the Camp Commandant, everybody in Japan works 10 days and rests on the eleventh, therefore we do the same.

On Wednesday, we were visited during lunch hour by a Japanese Major and other officials. It was rather surprising when he spoke in faultless English to a few of us. Judging by their personal appearance they appeared to have a strain of German blood in them.

Whether this is due to German immigration or German training I do not know. Also, the majority of women I have noticed in Japan bear children of the average age of 4–6 years old. It appears that they were ordered by the government to have more children.

Thursday we had a cigarette issue and also received a list of Japanese mining words which were translated into English. This list appears to bear out the rumour that we will go to work in the mines.

Sunday we had our rest day and we are catching up on our washing and sewing.

Well love, that is the finish of this weeks letter and the end of the month, so until next week, I'll say Au revoir and hope that your wishes and my wishes will speedily be answered.

Love Fred xx

7th February 1943

Dear Nola,

Once again I sit down to review the last week of activity and once again I hope that these weekly letters do not bore you.

The first day of February was rather warm and I regarded this as a happy omen for the future temperature of this cold and bleak village.

PART 2

The second day I worked until 4.50pm and was very glad to arrive back at the fire stove in the barracks.

On Wednesday, the camp and prisoners were inspected, during lunch hour, by a Japanese Lieutenant and also later in the afternoon whilst we were working.

Thursday we were detailed to clear the road, leading from Ohasi to Upper Ohasi, of a ten inch fall of snow. The work was easy but the 22 miles walk around the mountain was very gruelling.

The reason for this being our meals consist of a small bowl of rice and a small bowl of radish stew. Needless to say, the first half-hour of work consumes most of the energy generated by those meals.

Friday evening we were issued with a packet of cigarettes, one flimsy, lady-size handkerchief and a small bundle of Nippon Times newspapers dated January 18th–23rd 1943.

As these were the first newspapers and magazines we had read for four months, they were eagerly scanned. Although they were full of anti-allied propaganda, we were mighty pleased to read about the Allied Force fighting 40 miles West of Tripoli, and also the invasion of Algiers and Morocco.

The majority of men now hope to be free by Christmas

and the morale of the men is higher.

On Saturday I stayed back in the barracks because of a strained back caused by lifting large rocks.

On Sunday the weather was abominable. The rain was torrential in its down-pour and very quickly the surrounding area was changed to thick mud and slush.

At 8am word was issued that there would not be any working party required, so the men commenced to catch up on washing and sewing clothes.

Imagine our chagrin when word was passed for a working party of 20 men. I was lucky, I never went.

That night, after our meal of rice and radish stew, we held a General Knowledge Quiz and spent quite an enjoyable hour around the fire.

Well my elusive girl, I think that finishes the news for the time being, so you will have to be patient until next week.

One piece of news I forgot, was: last Monday we were issued with pay-books and when we start off for work we hand the books into the Japanese Office where they are stamped.

That night we were issued cigarettes and hanky. The persons who had no stamps in their book only received a half packet of cigarettes and no handkerchief.

Well my love the time is now 9.30am and the temperature is 22° Fahrenheit. I'm sitting down writing this diary and I can imagine you, busy at the salon and working in 90° to 100° Fahrenheit heat.

My, how I pine for that beautiful land of Australia.

Hoping that we'll be reunited in the near future I say Au revoir and best of everything

Love Fred xx

14th February 1943

Dear Nola,

After reviewing the week gone by, it appears to be rather a hectic week when compared with other weeks.

Monday I was unwell, so I stayed indoors. Around about 9am, the air raid alarms were sounded and later that evening, the Japanese Sergeant told us that many planes had bombed Mariana and killed many soldiers.

Tuesday I went to work and on arriving back, I learned

that a Japanese soldier had told the boys that Japan had issued Peace Terms to America but America had refused.

Wednesday I observed that the Japs around here were very sour. Whether it was due to the bombing or a further group of men had been called up, I do not know. One thing I do know is that the rationing is very strict and in cases of luxuries such as curry powder and pipes, etc, there are none. Sugar is rationed at 80 grams per month.

Thursday 11th was the Anniversary of the Emperor Meiji. The 2604th year of reign, so we had a holiday. In the morning our shell-struck Nippon Sergeant paraded before us with half a dozen medals on his chest.

Friday I learnt that the Dutch and Javanese prisoners were

February 11
Kenkoku Kinenbi – National Foundation Day

According to the ancient myths, on this date in 660 BC the Japanese Nation was founded by Emperor Jimmu. February 11th is also the date that the Meiji Constitution was proclaimed. Because of these connections to the Emperor Worship system the Occupation cancelled the Foundation Day, but the Japanese government reinstated it in 1966. In most cities various groups take to the streets and demonstrate against the revival of the Imperial system.

going home to Java in April because the Dutch puppet Government had signed Peace with Japan.

Saturday I worked up the hill, clearing snow from the roads.

Sunday a further batch of uniforms for the Dutch arrived.

Love Fred xx

21st February 1943

Dear Nola,

Like the eternal brook, I keep on bubbling on.

This week was rather uneventful as far as outstanding news goes but I'll make it sound as interesting as possible.

On Monday the weather was rather warm, so it wasn't bad working outdoors. Our job was to collect sticks of wood.

Judging by the amount of wood they burn and use for building purposes, I'm sure that there will be a serious shortage of timber in this country within the next five years.

When the Japanese erect a building, the timber arrives

already cut and measured so all the Japs do is, assemble the building according to blue-prints. Practically all buildings in Ohasi are of similar type so one set of blue-prints could be used for all buildings. The timber used is very green, so in time, the wood warps and cracks appear everywhere. Another peculiar feature of their buildings is that the buildings are constructed so that they can be disassembled with the shortest of time and labour.

The Japanese electrical system is rather old fashioned and their equipment is very poor.

Tuesday night I received my first pay in Nippon. The huge amount of 260 cents out of which 150 was deducted for a rubber stamp.

Thursday, the camp was visited by a Japanese Lt. Colonel and 20 journalists.

Friday and Saturday I didn't work, and on Sunday we were officially told that POW postcards were in the Commandant's office, and that we might have a chance to write home soon. Also we might receive Red Cross parcels.

Needless to say, we are interested and looking forward to the time when we can write home.

As the days and weeks go by I'm always thinking and

imagining how you are. It will be fun to look back over these days once we are together again. Just to be with you, behind the wheel of a fast car and to hear you sing.

Well my love, I think that finishes the scandal for the time being so until later I say Au revoir with lots of love.

Fred xx

28th February 1943

Dear Nola,

The weather is extremely cold as I write this letter so excuse the scribble.

Monday started the week with Yours Truly carrying logs at the sawmill, and I was very glad when the day's work was finished.

Tuesday I was on the job of carrying pipes weighing about 250 lbs. As three persons carried these pipes approximately 300 yards, I was more than glad when that day was finished.

Wednesday was on the logs again and when I came back to the barracks I learnt that we would be moving to the new camp on the 20th March.

Thursday evening I received two pencils off the Japanese when we marched in from work.

Friday was another working day and on Saturday I went to the electrician shop for a trade test.

Saturday and Sunday I worked at the electrician shop.

PS: Excuse the abrupt finish.

Love Fred xx

Working party bringing fallen tree trunks to timber mill in Ohasi

7th March 1943

Dear Nola,

Today officially starts the beginning of spring in Japan but I can truthfully say that the weather is as cold as an iceberg. During the day I worked at the electrician shop, winding a coil for an electric magnet.

Tuesday I did similar work. Later that day I learnt that the Japanese Commandant was going to tell us good news.

After tea, the Commandant told us that we would be allowed to write home once a month. Later on we were issued with a letter-card and also a list of forbidden subjects we weren't allowed to write about.

Needless to say I asked Norm MacNab to let you know that I'm OK and looking forward to the day when we would be re-united. The date I sent the card was March 2nd 1943.

Wednesday my dear elusive girl, I went back to the new schedule at the electricians shop.

Thursday, Friday, Saturday and Sunday were more or less the same, the weather still cold.

Well my love that finishes the news for the time being so until later on I'll say Au revoir hoping and wishing that all your wishes come true in the shortest possible time.

Love Fred xxx

PS. I often wonder how "Freddie" is progressing.

> *"Freddie" was Nola's scotch terrier dog.*

SAFE AND WELL

When you're sucking at your pencil

And you don't know what to say

When you wish the flaming censor

Had ne'er seen the light of day

There's always one small item left, we know to tell

It doesn't take much writing, saying -

"Dear Mum, I'm safe and well."

Though the tucker may be "oncus"

The water pretty crook

We haven't seen a drop of beer

Since Wavell took Tobruk

You've been before the Skipper for being AWL

But take your pen and write it down,

"Dear Mum, I'm safe and well."

We heard German bombers often

Come thundering overhead,

and it isn't very pleasant

To be dodging lumps of lead

And as we manoeuvre in and out

'Midst hail of shrapnel and shell

We still have time to send a line

"Dear Mum, I'm safe and well."

A lone Mum or Mother stands

Beside the old bush track

Is waiting for the mailman

For news of her sailor - Jack

A smile lights up her care-worn face

With a beauty no words can tell

When she reads the old familiar words

"Dear Mum, I'm safe and well."

14th March 1943

Dear Nola,

Once again I review another week of prison life and except for one or two incidents, the week was similar to past weeks.

Needless to say the weather is still cold and now that we aren't issued with any coal, the time elapsing between 4 o'clock, when we finish work, until when we have roll-call, 8 o'clock at night, is very cool. The majority of us go to bed as soon as roll-call is over. If anybody had told me during peace time that in the future I would be going to bed at 8 o'clock of a night, I would have said that they were mad, but such is the case.

As I lay in bed I often picture in my mind what I think you would be doing and it gives me encouragement to carry on until I am home again with you. It is hard to realise that it is over a year since I was with you and I fervently wish that you are in the best of health and happiness.

When I notice how the Japanese women live, I hope and pray to God that such a plight will never befall the women of Australia. Food is very scarce, and clothing is the same.

The most remarkable thing about conditions in Japan is: although the population in this part of Japan all eat at community eating houses and live in community houses, one family to two rooms, and that the women work twice as hard in the mines as an ordinary miner would in Australia, on the surface they appear contented. Whether this is due to ignorance or a fanatical spirit, I do not know.

I talk with the Jap man in charge of the electric cars for the mine. One thing I am convinced of is that they are sick of war as much as we are, if not more, because everything is very strictly rationed and in cases of milk, eggs, fruit, sugar, salt and cigarettes they are practically non existing.

Well my elusive girl, to return to the present day life, I am still working at the electricians shop doing odd jobs etc.

On Friday the twelfth, we were inspected by the Chief Commandant of the Hakodate Prison Camps and later the same afternoon we had a ceremonial parade outside the barracks. One American soldier was presented with a diploma in Japanese and English writing to the effect that he was a willing and diligent worker whilst a Nipponese prisoner. He was also presented with a parcel of ten packets of cigarettes and two tins of pears.

Saturday, a detail of men were sent down to the station to bring back boxes of stuff. Later that day, the rumour spread to the effect that there were Red Cross clothing and articles in those boxes. So far we haven't heard anything official.

Saturday evening we were told to re-write our letter-cards as the previous cards had been refused by the censors because the writing was too small. So this time we were limited to twelve lines for the actual text of the message.

Today, Sunday, is Yasmi day or rest day, so I spent most of the day diligently snoring in bed. Which is not a bad idea in this cold country.

Well my love, the latest rumour is that Turkey has declared war on Germany, but as we have no way of confirming the rumour, we can only wait and hope that the news is correct. A paragraph in the latest issue of Nippon Times states that Germany and Italy have recalled their Ambassadors to Turkey and that Turkey's and England's Prime Ministers held a meeting, so it is quite feasible that Turkey has declared war.

> During World War II, Turkey signed a peace treaty with Germany and officially remained neutral until near the end of war. In 1945 Turkey joined the UN, and in February 1945 it declared war on Germany and Japan.

Well, until next letter, I'll leave you hoping that I'm in a position to show you these letters in the near future. So until then, I'll say Au revoir,

Love Fred xx

PS: Kind regards to Mr and Mrs Caldwell, and a juicy bone to "Freddie".

21st March 1943

Dear Nola,

Like the Income Tax inspector, here I am again and I'm feeling extra well.

The weather of late has been rather mild, the temp; averaging 40°–50° but to spoil the effect, it has been raining fairly steadily.

The week started off with Yours Truly working at the electricians shop winding electro-magnet field coils, a nice comfortable easy job by a fire.

In this particular shop, there are 20 Japanese and 12 of us. The Japanese are either returned men from the war or men who cannot do heavy work. From what I can deduct from this Iron Ore Mining Company, all men that are strong are employed in the mine, doing the actual mining. Those who have accidents, or are too weak are withdrawn from the mine and are employed as a technician such as electrician, welder, mechanic or some other trade incidental to the mine. Firstly they are given two months training at a Technical School and then left to learn by the trial of experience.

If the Japanese make a bad mistake at their work, they nearly have a fit of hysterics and after finishing laughing, they calmly toss the object aside. The way they go about a job makes a man shudder. The main weapon or tool of a Japanese tradesman is a hammer. The way they use a hammer on fairly light materials would get them instantaneous dismissal back home.

The most remarkable thing about it is that after smacking and hammering at the different machines they are employed on, the darn thing eventually goes. Whether they possess a sixth sense or are very lucky, I do not know, but such is the results.

Well my love, Tuesday evening, a party of men were detailed to bring back seventeen cases of tinned pineapple from the railway station. You can imagine our thoughts as to whether we were going to be issued with fruit, or what would happen.

Thursday and Friday evening, word was passed around, that fruit, pepper, curry, socks, pads and pencils would be on sale at the Commandant's Office. The prices were; fruit 50c, pepper 15c & 30c a pkt & bottle, curry 15c, socks 50c, pads 10c and pencils 5c. Most of the articles were quickly bought by the prisoners who, by a strange coincidence, were paid the previous evening for their working days during the month of February.

There was a rumour that the items sold to us should have been issued to us but nothing official has been heard.

Saturday, we were notified that we would be moving to the new camp, at the end of the month.

We are to do our own cooking down there so five men comprising of one American sailor, one American soldier, one English RAF, one Chinaman and one Australian and also five Dutchmen.

The Commandant told the Dutch Officer that down at the new camp we would most likely receive increased food rations which would include meat and sometimes chicken. The reason for this being, that at present we are fed at the Mine's kitchen, whilst at the new camp we will be fed under military conditions.

The Commandant also said that the canteen would most likely be resumed and as the different stores would arrive from Kamaiski, we would most likely have a fairly large variety of items to choose from.

Well my elusive girl, I think that finishes the news for the time being, so today being "Yasme" day, or rest day, I'll bid you Au revoir and wish you the best of everything,

love Fred xx
PS: I think I'll do some washing and then get to bed.

28th March 1943

Dear Nola,

Once again I look back on another week of prison life and try and record some of the incidents that took place.

During Monday and Tuesday, we were inspected by a visiting Japanese Captain whilst at our various occupations. As luck would have it, I appeared very industrious when the visitors arrived at the Electrician or Dinki shop. The work at the shop is still congenial and as we are more or less left alone by the Japs, life isn't so bad after all.

Wednesday and Thursday were similar to other days and on Friday evening we were allowed to buy two packets of cigarettes per man, at 15c per packet. A few of the men doubled up for a second issue but received a few smacks over the head and body with a wooden sword they keep in the office.

Saturday and Sunday were ordinary working days, but on Friday afternoon we were ordered to go to the hospital to receive an injection, for tuberculosis I believe, and also a regular examination. We had to strip down to a pair of underpants and wait in a cold draughty hall until it was your turn to be examined. Boy Oh Boy we nearly froze and were mighty glad to dress again.

Saturday evening about twelve of us who never get weighed, chest measured or temperature taken, were ordered down to the hospital again and once again we undressed in that very cold hall-way.

Sunday evening we were told that we would be working at the new camp in preparation for moving on April 1st. As the weather is still cold we don't like the idea of moving but orders are orders, so tomorrow I'll start packing my scanty gear. The Japanese told us that we would receive an increased food ration, so if that is the case, the new camp might not be so bad after all.

Well my love that finishes the news for the time being, so until further news I finish this letter hoping that you are in the best of health and spirits. So once again I say Au revoir and keep smiling.

Love Fred xx

4th April 1943

Dear Nola,

Well my elusive girl, it is over fourteen months since I last saw your smiling face and it seems years since I had my last dance with you.

Unless my memory is faulty, the last dance was at Earl's Court. It will be great when Norm MacNab, you and I can once again go to different dances again. I often wonder whether Norm is engaged or even married. Gosh, I'll rag him if he is married.

Well, this week commenced with the usual work at the Dinki shop, but I'm glad to relate, the day was a beautiful sunny day. Seeing that the day was sunny, the Nips had a roaring fire going in the store. Funny people you say! I'll say.

Wednesday we went to the new camp and prepared the camp for our change over. The following day, April 1st of all days, the fools, meaning us, carted our luggage to the new camp, a distance of 1³/₄ miles. As we did two trips with our own luggage and another trip to clean the vacated barracks, my poor feet were pretty sore, but such is life.

For dinner and tea we were fed from the new camp

kitchen and although the rice was doughy and the stew was soya sauce and green leaves, the ration was extra good. Approximately twice as much as we received at the old camp, so we were more or less satisfied.

On Friday 2nd the food ration was little more than normal but as we had an extra 2 $\frac{1}{2}$ miles to walk each day, the outlook was not good.

Saturday, we rose at 6am for tinko, or morning roll call, ten minutes for exercise, wash, then breakfast. After breakfast we filled up our lunch boxes, we had received the previous evening, and then fell in on the parade ground at 7.40am.

We arrived at work at roughly 8.15am, worked until 11.15am, had lunch in the sun until 12.45pm and finished work at 4pm, thence home, and then we ate.

Today, Sunday, is Yasme day, and most of the boys, including Yours Truly, catch up with washing and mending.

The latest rumour is that Turkey is definitely in the war on our side, that the Nips have evacuated the Solomons and New Guinea, and that heavy fighting is occurring in Burma and Timor. How true the rumours are we don't know, but it sure cheers a man up.

> Evacuation of over 11,000 Japanese troops from Guadalcanal, Solomon Islands, was completed by 8th February 1943. Fighting was still going on in New Guinea, Burma and Timor.

Well my love, I think that finishes the news for the time being so once again I say Au revoir and best of luck.

Love Fred xx

11th April 1943

Dear Nola,

This week started with a new routine. The day began with "tinko" at 5am, we fill our lunch boxes and at 5.55am, we have a roll call. After roll call we have 10 minutes to exercise, then breakfast.

At 7.20am we parade for work and after numerous bowing and saluting, off we go to work. When we arrive at Ohasi, we have more bowing and scraping, and thence to work. Dinner at 11.30am until 12.30pm, thence finished at 4.30pm and once again bowing and saluting. Tea at 5.30pm, tinko at 7.30pm and then to bed. That finishes the day.

On Tuesday, the Japanese miners and workers held a farewell meeting for the soldiers going away. Wednesday, we heard that Japan had been bombed. Here, the people were putting up blackout curtains, so the news seems to be correct.

Friday we were paid for the previous month, so I am rich again by the princely sum of 2.70 cents, about 5/6d in our money.

Friday afternoon, a train load of Japanese forced labour men arrived in Ohasi by train. These men will work in the mine.

During the week we were issued with another bundle of newspapers and books by the Japanese. The date on the papers, was 26th February; the news was mostly about their success during the previous year.

Sunday was rather a warm day, which is a change. During the afternoon, a Japanese cut down a tree which fell against the high tension electric wires and caused them to short. There were Nips running everywhere and it was nearly two hours before the power was switched on again.

Well my love, that finishes the news for the time being, so until next week I'll say Au revoir,

Love Fred xx

18th April 1943

Dear Nola,

Once again I sit down to pen you another weekly letter and I hope that at the same time you are in the best of health.

This week was another week of dinki work and most of the work was on the mine's electric tractors.

On Friday 16th we were issued with rubber sand shoes and also we received a few chess sets and a table tennis outfit. All gifts from the Japanese YMCA. The Japanese also let us listen to their radio. We were told that we would be allowed to use the gifts and listen to the wireless on yasme days. The same day a party of us were detailed to collect firewood from the surrounding hills so as we could enjoy a bath every two nights.

On Saturday, 20 of the boys were sent to work at a lime quarry a few miles towards Kamaichi and 50 more were sent to work in the mines, starting at 2pm and finishing around midnight. According to the boys, the work is all right but the long walk is killing.

Well my love once again I must say how much I am amazed at the audacity of the Japanese in general. They do things and get away with it, which we would never dream of doing. For instance, they run 3,300 volts into the mines with terrible insulation and the transformers are stowed away on a couple of loose wooden boards. Their railways are narrow gauge and never built up on curves so it is a common occurrence to see six or seven trucks tipped up on the side of the lines. The amount of casualties that occur in Japan annually must be enormous. In the vegetable gardens, they use human fertiliser so if a person was fastidious about his food, he would starve. All work is done the same way as their forefathers did it hundreds of years ago. In fact if there were two ways of doing a job, the Japanese would do it the hardest way.

Well my elusive girl that is the end of the news for the time being, so until next letter I'll say best of luck and Au revoir.

Love Fred xx

25th April 1943

Dear Nola,

The weather of late has been getting warmer and warmer and the trees are bursting into bud. In a few weeks time the scenery should be very beautiful. Most of the flowering trees are cherry and persimmon trees.

This week, the Japs came to light with a work sheet. The

idea is that if our work isn't first-class, we would be transferred to a mine working party.

Thursday evening, the Japanese complained about the amount of vegetables that were disappearing from the kitchen.

Friday we moved an electric welding machine from the welding shop, to the Dinki Yama shop by railway truck. In the afternoon we brought the empty railway truck back by road. Talk about a rough ride. I'm sure only Japs would think of pushing a railway truck down a road, but such was the case.

Friday was also Good Friday but we worked as usual.

Saturday we were warned by the Japanese pole vaulter (a civilian soldier recruited to bolster the armed forces – not sure of the origin of the term) not to talk to any of the civilian Japanese. When we heard this we hoped that the Japanese were getting pushed back by the Allied Forces.

On Sunday, it was work as usual, but seeing that it was Easter Sunday and also Anzac Day, I stood to attention for two minutes.

On the way home from work we carried a few cases of biscuits from the railway station. The rumour is that they are for issue on the Emperor's Birthday on the 29th April.

Well my love, I think that finishes the news for the time being so until next week I'll say Au revoir and best of health and luck.

Love Fred xx

THE DENSHA SHOP

Dear Nola,

Once again I sit down and review the past week of events.

This week I went to work at the Densha, or Electric trolley shop overhauling the motors and wiring in general. As usual the type and quality of the material in the car is the usual poor Nippon quality.

Thursday, being the Emperor's birthday, we were allowed a yasme. The same day, Collins, an American sailor was sentenced to five days gaol on one meal a day, for smoking after "Tinko" (roll call).

Rommel had defeated the Allies in the Battle of Gazala *in June 1942 and captured Tobruk. His push was only halted at the Alamein Line on the border of Egypt in the* First Battle of El Alamein *(July 1942). General Bernard Montgomery took over as commander of the Eighth Army and after victory in the* Battle of Alam Halfa *(September 1942) and in the* Second Battle of El Alamein_*(October-November 1942) began to the push the Axis forces back, going as far as capturing* Tripoli *in January 1943.*

Saturday, we received some more newspapers dated the 26th March. The news was fairly good, especially the Western Desert Campaign.

Sunday, I started the job of copying out a Nippon-English Language book.

The most surprising thing about these Japs is the amount of sex maniacs. As the country is urging more babies, it appears that the authorities are very lax about sex matters.

The way the Jap men talk and make gestures in front of the girls would make anybody blush.

The living condition is very poor. Families are crowded into two room flats and every family usually has three or more babies. If our children were brought up under the same conditions, very few would survive the first two years.

Well my love, until next letter I'll say Au revoir and hope and wish that you are in the best of health and happiness.

Love Fred xx

9th May 1943

Dear Nola,

This week was a pretty eventful week. As usual the work has been on the Denshas.

On Wednesday a Korean miner was killed by a fall of rock and on Thursday one of the honourable pole vaulters or civilian soldiers was killed by a rock fall in the mine. The mining party was three hours late in arriving back to camp. Instead of arriving at 12 o'clock, they arrived back at 3am.

> *Earthquakes were very common in this part of Japan with one or two tremors a week being the average. These probably contributed to the rock falls.*

Owing to the death, the camp had a yasme on Friday and Saturday. On Sunday, ten of us were picked to go to the guard's funeral. The proceedings started at 1pm and lasted until 2pm. The guard's ashes were in a box standing on an altar, below the box was his photo. Three priests officiated the rites, two assists and the main priest. The assistant on the left would beat a cymbal and the assistant on the right would beat a gong. Then the three priests would go into a chant. While the chanting was going on, the mourners would salute the Colonel from Hakodate and then pay their respects to the deceased. When the rites were over, we were presented with four rice-cakes each and the following day we were charged 50 cents each for the privilege of attending the funeral. The excuse was that the money was for the incense that was burnt at the funeral. Monday they buried the box of ashes.

Well my love, until next letter, I say Au revoir.

Love Fred xx

16th May 1943

Dear Nola,

Having a few minutes to spare before I go to sleep, I'll sit down and write about the main events of the past week.

At 12 o'clock Sunday night, a crowd of 40 Englishmen from Hakodate, a Japanese island north of Tokyo, arrived at our camp. Although the food they received at Hakodate was quite sufficient, they were in poor health owing to the lack of clean clothes and lack of water for washing. The majority had skin diseases and quite a few were suffering from beri-beri. At Hakodate, the work was usually connected with ship-building.

Tuesday, thirty of our chaps, comprising three Australians,

nine Americans, four Englishmen, one Malayan and thirteen Dutchmen, were dispatched to Hakodate. (The three Australians were Jimmy Lea, Freddie George and Izzy Langford, all from Victoria).

On Wednesday, my elusive girl, a Korean miner was carried down the road on a stretcher. I believe that he was trapped by a fall of rock in the mine. Thursday the mine roof again caved in. Luckily, nobody was trapped.

Friday afternoon, our first batch of Red Cross parcels arrived. The parcels contained pudding, milk, chocolate, beef, sweets and soap. We were told that the parcels would be issued on the 20th, that day being a yasme day. Also, sugar, salt and cocoa came in bulk and starting from yasme day, we would be issued with cocoa at night-time.

The same afternoon (Friday) I had a bad attack of stomach pains. The trouble being bad fish in my lunch box. That evening I tasted my first piece of meat since I've been in Ohasi. The meat was bully beef supplied by the International Red Cross, and was enjoyed very much.

Saturday Evening I received my pay, the princely sum of 2 yen 60 sen.

Well my love it is nearly fifteen months since I was taken prisoner and since I've been in Nippon I have been amazed by the living conditions of the people here. The latrines are just a hole dug in the ground and at the present time, just covered in maggots. When they receive an issue of fish, they leave the fish out in the sun to dry and incidentally get fly-blown. No wonder thousands die of disease every year.

> *An interesting insight into the mind of the Japanese people is the need to show humility to the Emperor. For instance, once a month, even the manager of the mine would join with his employees in bailing out the railway toilets. They would fill a tanker with this smelly sewage, and it would be taken away to fertilize the vegetable gardens.*

In Japan, the people have been taught thoroughly that it is a sin not to work and that all work should be done with a smile and without complaint, so it is not unusual to see men and women of all ages and conditions doing heavy manual work.

In the mines the men are injured every day and it's the injured person's own responsibility to fend for himself until he is well again.

Well my love, that finishes the news for the time being so until next letter I'll once again say Au revoir and best of wishes.

Love Fred xx

PS: Think of the good times we'll have when we get together again. Whoopee!

23rd May 1943

Dear Nola,

At the present moment we have been ordered to do physical exercise but I'm taking a chance and writing this letter.

Well my girl, this week was another week of work on the Denshas. I've been given the job of rewiring the lighting and power panel on the Denshas and the work is very interesting.

One of the young Nippon electricians, 18 years of age, is compelled to attend a military parade three nights a week. The hours are 3.30pm–6.30pm. The parade is held at the local school. At the school the young kiddies are given toy swords and rifles and drilled on genuine Nippon army drill. Also, there are boys of 18 years age, driving locomotives and doing other man size jobs.

The buildings around here are very poor. After the buildings have been completed, the wood begins to strain and warp in every kind of way the result being a sagging building.

At the present time the hillsides are covered in flowering trees and the view is very nice. There is one type of flower somewhat similar to our honey-suckles and often I have noticed the children eating these flowers.

Saturday, a few of the boys presented the foreman of the machine shop with sugar and on the following day he returned the gift in the form of pork stew.

Well my love that concludes the news for the time being so I'll say Au-revoir,

Love Fred xx

30th May 1943

Dear Nola,

As there isn't much in the way of news this week, I'm afraid this letter will be very short.

As usual I spent another week of work at the Densha.

To break the monotony, I have been doing odd jobs in the mine; mostly repairing electric trolleys.

During the week, one of the Japanese electricians, age 24, was killed whilst working on 3300V wires. He was repairing a faulty join and received a shock. The shock threw him to the ground 25 feet below. He was killed instantaneously. The following day, the electrician's staff were given half a day's holiday so as to attend the funeral.

Well my love that finishes the news for the time being, "and as the weather is still good" being the only other news I can impart, I'll end up by wishing you the best of everything.

Love Fred xx

6th June 1943

Dear Nola,

This week was the same as last week except for one important thing, but that I'll touch on later in the letter.

As usual I'm still working at the Densha and trips now and then up to the mine. The weather is fine and getting warmer day by day. In a few weeks time I hope to go swimming at a small dam near the Densha-shop during lunch hour. Monday afternoon, the locomotive ran off the railway lines but only small damage resulted. Tuesday morning, several railway trucks loaded with ore left the railway lines and except for two trucks getting smashed up, the damage was slight.

Wednesday, I learnt that 20,000 American soldiers, assisted by numerous aircraft and ships, captured 2600 Japanese soldiers on the Luzon Islands.

Saturday, the nation was in mourning because the Grand Admiral of the Japanese Navy had committed suicide at 11.15am the previous day (Friday 4th). At 11.15am on Saturday the Japanese stood bowed in silence for two minutes in remembrance. Needless to say, the news caused much glee among us, for we believe that the Japanese Navy has sustained a serious blow somewhere.

Well my elusive girl, I once again say good-night, so until next letter, I leave you thinking of the time when we will be together again.

Love Fred xx

20th June 1943

Dear Nola,

Having time to spare I have taken the opportunity to pen a few more lines about our daily existence.

This week was similar to other weeks; the weather is fine, the work fairly congenial and the usual amount of bashings from the guards.

Monday evening a Japanese civilian was run over by the train at the station and instantaneously killed, whilst at "=Si hi Yama, "the lime quarry", a Japanese fell off a cliff and landed 200 ft below on the rocks. Needless to say he was quite dead.

Wednesday, the Camp Commandant, Lt. Nagamura was summoned by telegram to an important conference at Hakodate, the headquarters of the prison camps in this part of Japan. So far he hasn't returned.

We learnt from the Japs that the population is eating the last of last year's rice and that an order abolishing the keeping of animals and birds except for farming purposes was issued.

I am inclined to believe that there is a very serious shortage of food in the country and owing to the strict submarine warfare in these waters, the Japs cannot import rice or other food commodities from occupied countries. I also heard that the Jap army in China are in a very bad way because of lack of aircraft whilst the allied forces have many aircraft.

After working with Japanese technicians for four months and using their equipment, I realise why Japanese equipment is useless. If the same quality of work and materials are in their war supplies, I can only pity the Jap who has to use them.

As I have said before, the main implements of a Jap technician is a hammer and chisel so I leave the results to your imagination.

Well my love, I feel pretty confident that the War will be nearly ended or ended by Christmas 1943.

It will be wonderful when we are together again and enjoying ourselves like we did during the good old days.

Well my love, that finishes the news for the time being so I'll say Au-revoir and wish you the best of health and happiness,

Love Fred xx

11th July 1943

Dear Nola,

Once again I'll sit down to write another letter and once again news is brief.

The last few days the town of Ohasi has been invaded by Jap soldiers of the 81st Battalion. The work they are doing consists of laying telephone line from Ohasi to Kamaishi. Tuesday morning a Japanese civilian was run over by a gasoline car and severely injured. The same morning the Jap foreman of the Densha-shop, dropped a gear case on my fingers and I was sent to the hospital to have my hands attended to. Whilst there I saw the dead Jap, and a terrible sight he was. After the hospital, it was back to work. No matter how bad the injury, you must keep working.

Well my love, I think that finishes the news for the time being so until later I'll say Au revoir and best of wishes,

Love Fred xx

18th July 1943

Dear Nola,

At the present moment the weather is rather hot and I am stripped down to a pair of shorts.

Back home, at this particular period I imagine that you would be clothed in your winter woollies.

As usual, I'm still working at the Densha and I'm quite contented with the work.

On Monday, an Englishman from Hakodate Camp died of

lung trouble. The same evening we held a funeral service over the coffin, and then the body was taken away to be cremated. On the following morning, an Englishman and a Jap went to the Crematorium to collect the ashes and whilst there the Jap raked amongst the ashes so as to find the gold tooth belonging to the deceased. The same evening the ashes were buried in the Japanese grave-yard at the village of Omask.

Wednesday and Thursday went as usual, but on Friday Ross Drabble was beat up with a heavy stick by a Jap Orderly Officer. After nearly killing Ross, the Jap put Ross "under arrest" and had him locked up in the gaol.

The following evening, we were called out on parade and told that Drabble had been sentenced to five days gaol for "escaping from parade."

Sunday was another working day and as nothing unusual happened on that day, I'll bring this letter to a close hoping that you are still in the best of health.

Love Fred xx

25th July 1943

Dear Nola,

As I sit down to write this letter, my mind is full of disgust as to the living conditions of the Japanese people.

For the last few weeks, the weather has been fairly warm and consequently the Japanese people, women in particular have been discarding their surplus clothing and having the doors and windows of their pig-sties, I mean homes, open.

At present the women go around half naked and dirty, the children are similar and in some cases, worse. The interior of their homes look and smell like pig-sties.

I'm certain that whilst I have a voice, or pair of hands at my command, I'll do my utmost to stop our living standard from descending to the low level of the Japanese.

To continue the letter, I'm working at the Densha as usual and except for the increasing number of break-downs on the denshas due to the lack of proper parts for replacements, there isn't anything unusual to report from there.

On Tuesday a notice was issued to the Japanese people that all men between the ages of 15 years to 41 years, had to report for a physical examination. Whether this notice is because there is a shortage of fighting men for the Army or whether it is an annual check-up, I do not know.

I also heard that Allied troops had landed in Sicily, and that Italy was surrendering fast. I was also told by a Jap that the Americans had landed and captured Java. Personally I don't believe the last piece of news, but I'm mighty bucked up over the Italian news.

Well my love, that finishes the news for the time being so until next letter I'll leave hoping that you are in the best of health and happiness.

Love Fred xx

PS: Give my regards to Mr & Mrs Caldwell and give "Freddie" a juicy bone.

2nd August 1943

Dear Nola,

Once again I sit down to write a letter with your ever-refreshing memory before me.

Time and time again during my daily work, I think of all the good times we had together before this accursed war overcame world peace. This village of Ohasi being one hour in time behind Melbourne, I always imagine what you would be doing at that particular instance.

For instance, at this particular moment it is seven o'clock Monday 2nd August and I imagine that you would either be seeing a picture show or resting at home with Freddie.

Well my elusive girl, to get back to the news.

This week was similar to past weeks. The usual number of accidents in the mine, and the weather is still fairly warm.

On Wednesday we received Nippon newspapers written in English and the outstanding news is that Allied troops have landed on Italian islands and Sicily and Italy itself is being heavily bombed. Also, Allied troops are massing on the Turkey-Syrian border waiting for Turkey to declare war on Germany.

Well my love, I also heard that Mussolini and his cabinet had resigned and Marshall Bagdiello had taken over. If this is true I can expect the news of Italy's capitulation any day.

Seeing that about finishes the news I'll draw this letter to an end by hoping and praying that the war will be over by Christmas time and I'll be home by March or April 1944.

Love Fred xx

15th August 1943

Dear Nola,

Having a few minutes to spare in my rather crowded working routine, I'll take the opportunity to record the last fortnight.

At present the Mining Company's officials have had posters erected around the town. On these posters are recorded the daily efficiency percentage of the different Nippon labour Corps. The majority are around 80%.

We are still hearing rumours about the war situation in Europe and the South Pacific. Having no definite news I can only hope for the best.

On Monday 9th August, two American sick bay naval orderlies and an American Army surgeon doctor arrived at the camp and after hearing about the conditions of other prison camps in Japan, I'm sure that this camp isn't the worst camp by a long way. On the 13th we were told that an International Red Cross official would arrive at the camp and investigate the conditions in general. Previous to this on yasme day the 10th, we were issued with a complete set of Nippon clothes with rain-coat, as well as some English books.

On 14th we tidied the barracks and grounds up and went to work wearing our new rain-coats.

At 8am that day the official arrived, the official proving to be a Swiss.

The official met with representatives from the camp: Captain Zeigler represented the Americans, Sgt Major Ward the Australians, and Bill Marshall for the English. The official was only allowed to ask five questions, which were:

(1) Is the food alright?
(2) The living conditions O.K?
(3) Have you benefited by the Red Cross?
(4) Have you received letters? and
(5) What do you need most?

Captain Zeigler's answers to these questions were:

(1)   The food at the present moment is OK.
(2)   The living conditions were OK.
(3)   We have so far received one issue of Red Cross parcels per man.
(4)   We haven't received any letters, although we have written two.
(5)   Food and medicine.

The Swiss Official said "At the present moment there are

over 500,000 letters being sorted by a staff of officials in Tokyo, working 24 hour shifts."

Well my elusive girl, I think that finishes the news for the time being, so until further news I'll say Au-revoir and best of wishes.

Love Fred xx

PS: *Give my warmest regards to your father and mother and a nice juicy bone for "Freddie".*

22nd August 1943

Dear Nola,

At present the weather is terrible and the rain is pouring down in bucketfuls and the creeks are in flood. On the mountain side trees and rocks are sliding down. Whilst in Ohasi, the high tension wires (33,000V) blew together and shorted out, and owing to faulty switch mechanism in the power station, the wires burnt through before the switch opened.

Things in general are very quiet and nothing outstanding has happened.

On Wednesday 18th approximately 50 men had severe

pains in the stomach and after examination by the American doctor, the cause was blamed on food poisoning. With so many persons sick, the Commandant decided that the following day be a yasme.

After a rather peaceful day we were told to go to work the following day and the sick numbered only 30 men.

As a result of this, our diet consisted of rice and soya water for soup. After three days of this diet we went back to our usual diet, a bowl of rice and watery vegetable soup. Well my love that finishes the news for the time being, so until next letter, Au revoir,

Love Fred xx

29th August 1943

Dear Nola,

Having a few minutes to spare I'll take the opportunity to pen down a few of the local happenings.

As usual I'm still working at the Densha repairing the cars. The most outstanding thing regarding the maintenance of the cars is the absolute lack of spare parts. If an object cannot be repaired it is done without.

This week one of the American sailors, Stoddart by name, contracted appendicitis and was operated on at the Ohasi hospital. The operation was performed by the American doctor and was quite a success.

Apart from that the week was uneventful so I'll pass on to the following week.

AN ESCAPE

Dear Nola,

Today Monday the 30th August and a yasme day is rather an exciting day in our rather dull life, the reason being that an English air-force prisoner has escaped. When we filled in on the parade ground for morning roll call we found out that everybody was on parade including the cooks. When I noticed this I knew that something was wrong and after the roll call had proceeded it was ascertained that an Englishman was missing.

This news staggered the Japs and sent them into a panic, and after questioning a few of the boys who slept near him, the Japs found out that the escapee had forced an entrance into the kitchen and had a meal of potatoes and chicken.

After the Japs had ascertained as to what type of clothes the prisoner was last seen wearing, they loaded their rifles and climbed into the motor-cycle and sped off to Karmaichi.

Around about 5pm that same day, the escapee was marched into the camp and locked up in the gaol. His search party consisted of the police, soldiers, fire-brigade and many civilian searchers. Judging by the appearance of the searchers, it appeared that the search was conducted through thick swampy bush but as the prisoner was captured, everybody was happy.

After a few minutes of explanation to the Commandant, the searchers were served with beer and after consuming the beer, the party left for their respective homes, and the camp went back to normal.

Well my elusive girl, as far as the rest of the week goes there isn't much more to add, so rather than bore you I'll end by wishing you the best of happiness and health

Fred xxx

PS: Give my regards to everybody and a juicy bone to "Freddie".

12th September 1943

Dear Nola,

Like the ever babbling brook here I am again. This week was eventful for two things. The first is the number of accidents that have happened in the space of three or four days. On the Ohasi–Kamaishi railway line there has been four accidents in four days. The casualties being two men seriously injured and several slightly injured. Two out of the four accidents were caused by the train running off the line, which are 30 inch gauge. The third accident was a locomotive running off the lines owing to the points not being correctly positioned.

The fourth accident was due to a locomotive and trucks running into a stationary gasoline truck. In this accident one of the Japs was jammed between two trucks and had one leg cut off and the other broken.

The second and most important news was the capitulation of Italy.

Although we had heard rumours nothing was definite and it was a pleasant surprise when the Jap soldiers told us it was true. Due to Italy capitulating, the general opinion is that the European war will be well on its way to ending in three months time.

Personally speaking, I do not know how this will effect the European war, as our news is always at least a month old, so I can only hope for the best.

Needless to say, the news has put everybody in a good humour and some of the boys are even making plans for their first celebrations. If I can be home for the 1944 Easter I will be quite satisfied so I'll hope for the best.

Well my love that finishes the news for the time being so until next letter I'll say Au revoir,

Fred xx

19th September 1943

Dear Nola,

Having a few minutes to spare before lights out I'll take the opportunity to write a few words about the recent week.

As usual I'm working at the Densha overhauling the cars, and I'm still amazed over the fact that the cars continue to function although the replacement parts are mainly rubbish.

The weather at present is pretty decent although gradually getting colder day by day. According to the local Japs, they think that winter this year will be three to four weeks earlier and so, they are gathering in the winter firewood now. Well my love, I'm still in good health and always thinking of you, so until I hear of further news I'll say Au revoir and best of wishes,

Love Fred xx

26th September 1943

Dear Nola,

To continue from last letter.

The weather at the present moment is wet and cold. Owing to the intense rain there have been no wood parties for the bath, for the last six or seven days, therefore our bi-daily baths have been reduced to two baths in ten days.

There have also been a lot of landslides along the railway line and road-ways.

On Thursday 23rd I prayed to God for thanksgiving for looking after you and me. The occasion marked eighteenth months since I last prayed to God to help me when I was in the solitary cell in Serang.

Well my love, I hope it isn't long before I am with you and I can hear your voice, dance and do all the things we used to do. Surely it was only a short period ago when we were together at the different dances, or walking in the gardens, beaches and other places on a Sunday afternoon. I can well remember the first dance I had with you at Frankston. I often laugh when I think of the duel of wits between us on that night.

Well my elusive girl I think that finishes the news for the time being, so once again I say best of wishes and Au-revoir.

Love Fred xx

3rd October 1943

Dear Nola,

I have heard that two of the Americans and one Dutchman have received letters from their homes so I'm looking forward for the first letter and photo from you.

At night I often lay back and imagine whether you are still the same or more beautiful, and always promise that when I eventually arrive home again, and I find you willing, I will try to make you the happiest girl on earth. Gee, I have started off pretty mushy.

To arrive back at ordinary affairs. Owing to the rather heavy and persistent rain over the last week or two, the ground has become very loose and treacherous, so it wasn't very surprising when the news came through that the roof in the top mine had collapsed and killed three Koreans and injured five more. The following day the men were buried and their work mates were told to work at a different level.

Well my love except for the usual routine there is nothing else to report, so I'll end this short letter by wishing you the best of everything.

Love Fred xx

4th October 1943

Dear Nola,

Today is Monday the 4th of October and it is a very beautiful day indeed. The sun is shining and the trees, creeks and scenery in general are very beautiful.

Today is your birthday and naturally my thoughts are about you. The time at present is 7 o'clock in the evening and the corresponding time in Melbourne is 6 o'clock. I'm wondering whether you are preparing to leave for a dance or party in honour of your 22nd birthday. If you are I hope that you feel that I am with you in spirit and fervently wish that I was with you in flesh.

Well my elusive girl, regarding the local news of Ohasi, there isn't anything startling to relate; I'm working my usual routine at the Densha, the average number of accidents are happening around the mining area, and although there is the average number of accidents occurring, there hasn't been any fatalities.

Love Fred xx

11th October 1943

Dear Nola,

Today, Sunday 11th Oct, one of the air-compressors for the mine pushed the piston through the end plate of the cylinder and made a hole 18″ in diameter. The damage was so bad that the head man of the mine visited the compressor room and after inspecting the damage, ordered the broken part to be taken to Kamaishi for repairs.

One o'clock today, Elvie the Englishman who escaped from the camp was taken away to an unknown destination. According to the Japanese guards, he has been removed to Hakodate for inquiry into his escape and for sentence.

Well my elusive girl, that finishes the news for the time being, so until next letter I'll say Au Revoir and best of wishes.

Love Fred xx

24th October 1943

Dear Nola,

Once again I sit down to pen you a few lines regarding the current happenings of the previous week.

Often the letters are quite concise. This is due to the fact that they had to be written surreptitiously without the guards knowing. Because of the poor lighting in the barracks, they could not be written at night. Therefore, the only time available was the brief daylight period after dinner. The diaries had to be kept hidden, and mention very few names for fear of repercussions if they were found by the Japanese.

Group photo outside Japanese Guard Barracks
– Ohasi POW Camp

On Wednesday 20th, which was our day of rest, or as the Japanese would say, "Yasme Day", the Japanese Commandant presented us with musical instruments. The instruments consisted of a piano-accordion, two mouth organs, a kettle drum and last but not least, a violin. As luck would have it, we had amongst the prisoners plenty of men who are musically inclined and better still who could play the different instruments, so it wasn't many minutes before the men were practising tunes on the different instruments. That night, in honour of the arrival of the instruments a concert was quickly arranged and the same evening the patients in the hospital were entertained by song, music and dancing.

Well my love I'll have to finish this letter hoping it won't be very long before we are together again so until next week I say Au-revoir and best of cheer.

Love Fred xx

31st October 1943

Dear Nola,

As I sit down and write this letter I find it very hard to realise that it is over 21 months since I last saw you. Every night while I lay in bed I dream of you and I'm sure that if I were gifted so, I could paint your features true to life. Many a time I mentally review the different things we seen and did and many a laugh I get when I think of the different silly things we said and carried out. Often I promise myself that, when I arrive back in Australia I hope that we will be able to carry on where we were forced to discontinue.

Regarding the local happenings there isn't very much to say, so hoping that I will not bore you with the details I will commence.

I am working at the Denshas as usual and as the days go by the shortage of spare parts in Nippon becomes more and more transparent.

What spare parts we manage to receive are very poor in quality. The bolts in particular, being made of soft iron and other rubbish.

Well my elusive girl, I think that finishes the news for the time being so until further news I'll say Au-revoir.

Love Fred xx

7th November 1943

Dear Nola,

This week is rather barren of outstanding news so I'll cut this letter very short.

At the present time the weather is rather cold. During the day the average temperature is 45° to 50° Fahrenheit and at night, 34° to 40° Fahrenheit.

On Monday night before roll call, the Japanese Sergeant announced that "Elbie", the Englishman who attempted to escape had been tried by court-martial and found guilty. The sentence being 15 years in gaol. How they expect to keep him in gaol for 15 years, when I'm sure the war will be ended well before the end of 1944, I'm sure I don't know, but that is another example of how the minds of Japanese military men work.

On Monday 1st Nov., I celebrated my 25th birthday by staying in the camp and resting all day. I completely finished reading a book during the day. In honour of the occasion, I finished the last of my Red Cross packet which consisted of a tin of tomatoes. What a colossal meal.

Wednesday night, four of us received "radio-gram" forms, with instructions to the effect that we were allowed to write something personal to our kin-folk. The text of the message being limited to 40 words.

The reason given for this concession was that we were conscientious workers. What a sense of humour these Japanese have.

> *In actual fact, what we did in one day could be done in one hour. We were good actors and always looked like we were working. We always behaved ourselves, so we got away with it.*

As far as the rest of the week, I'm doing the usual routine work at the Densha and still wondering how the Denshas keep working.

> *Part of the wondering of how the Denshas kept working was because I had been pouring sulphuric acid onto the drive motor windings. Sulphuric acid was used as part of the soldering process. Unfortunately it was too dilute to cause any damage to the motor windings.*

Well my love, I think that covers the main news so until next letter I'll say Au-revoir and best of luck.

Love Fred xx

PS: Give my warmest regards to Mr & Mrs Caldwell and all your friends.

14th November 1943

Dear Nola,

At present the weather is very cold so I'll make this letter very brief.

I'm still working at the densha repairing their stupid electric cars. The more work I do on the cars, the more outstanding is the fact of the poor quality of the replacements. I'm convinced that in the near future the supply of spare parts will rapidly diminish and eventually the cars will stop running.
Recently, the mining officials tried to hurry the production rate, but owing to the sharp increase in injuries to the men working in the vicinity of the mine, the officials decided that the previous rate of production was all right.

Well my elusive girl, I think that finishes the news for the time being, so until further news, I'll say Au-revoir and best of luck.

Love Fred xx

28th November 1943

Dear Nola,

Once again I sit down to pen to you the daily events of the

last week.

At present the weather is very cold and as there aren't any fire stoves in the barracks the nights get very chilly. In answer to our questions regarding the installation of stoves, the Japanese Commandant replied – "Very shortly".

The news regarding my working days are similar to other weeks so I won't enlarge on that.

At present, practically all the prisoners are in good health, and out of the 164 prisoners in the camp, only four are really bad.

We received news that 200 Dutchmen and one Englishman had arrived in Karmaishi from Java. They received fairly good treatment on the trip over and only one person died. When they arrived in Japan there were only four slightly sick.

Well my love, that finishes the news for the time being, so until next letter I'll say Au-revoir and best of wishes.

Love Fred xx

P.S. Give my regards to everybody and a juicy bone to "Freddie".

12th December 1943

Dear Nola,

This week the news is similar to the previous week, so rather than bore you I'll make this letter very short.

The Dutch prisoners at Kamaishi are feeling the effects of the cold weather and the change in food. At the present time, seven have died and thirty-eight are in the hospital.

The Japanese soldier who is in charge of their kitchen is the worst kind of rogue, so I can understand why the food is upsetting the Dutchmen.

Further news is that the Nipponese Commandant has had five stoves installed in the barracks and that twelve truck loads of coal have arrived.

The food at present is fairly good. It consists of a bowl of rice and a bowl of vegetable soup for morning and evening meal. For lunch we have a bowl of rice and two or three small fish.

Well my elusive girl, once again I'll conclude this letter by hoping and wishing you the best of everything.

Love Fred xx

LETTERS ARRIVE

Dear Nola,

It is hard to realise that in a fortnight's time it will be Christmas 1943.

When I think back over the different Christmases I have enjoyed, the last two years seem like some fantastic nightmare. I fervently pray that the leaders of the different warring nations will take to heart the true message of Christmas and bring this war to a conclusion so as good cheer and love for thy fellow men will once more reign in the heart of all sensible people.

Well Nola, the outstanding news of this week is that approximately 120 letters arrived in the camp and although they were for the Americans and Dutch only, everybody was pleased that letters had eventually arrived.

The general tone of the letters is of hope and express the opinion that the war will be finished in 1944.

Not having any news regarding the European War, I can only place my faith in God and hope, God Willing, that the war will be over well before 1945 and that I celebrate the 1944 Christmas with you.

Until next letter I hope that you are in the best of heart and spirits,

Love Fred xx

26th December 1943

Dear Nola,

At present I am glancing at a few photos which my American friends have received from home. After seeing these more or less familiar scenes of home life and people, I must confess that I feel home sick.

One friend in particular received a photo of his two baby boys aged 2 years and 7 years respectively. The latest addition to the family he hasn't seen as he has been on Asiatic duty and a prisoner of war for the last 2 $\frac{1}{2}$ years. You can imagine his delight when he received the photos and letters.

On Christmas Eve, a Roman Catholic service was held around the stove at midnight. It was very beautiful.

On Christmas Day we were presented with approximately a pound of sugar and salt and cocoa donated by the British Red Cross.

At 10.30am a Church of England service was held in the new barracks and although we had no ordained preacher and the service was very simple, the feelings of the men who attended the service were very genuine.

Well my elusive girl, that finishes the news for the time being so until further news I'll say Au-revoir and a Merry Christmas and Happy New Year.

Love Fred xx

31st December 1943

Dear Nola,

Once again I'll try to pen down the happenings of the current week.

At the present time the weather is fairly cold, the average temperature being around 25° Fahrenheit, but as most of us work indoors and in access to a fire, we do not feel the cold biting winds howling outside. When the day's work is over and we return to the camp, there are five fires merrily burning, so once again we remain warm. If these conditions remain throughout the winter, I'm sure that we won't have anything to complain about.

Regarding the work, things are more or less unchanged. Daily I proceed to the Densha shop and repair their denshas. The average number of accidents occur daily with a fatal case once a week.

In our camp there is a slight outbreak of pneumonia but everything is under control. The latest news from Kamaishi prison camp is that 10 men have died and 45 are sick in hospital.

Well my elusive girl friend, I think that concludes the news for the time being, so until next letter I'll say Au-revoir and best of wishes.

Love Fred xx

PS: Give my warmest regards to your Father and Mother and a nice juicy bone to "Freddie".

3rd January 1944

Dear Nola,

Today is the first weekly letter of the New Year, and looking back on last year's weekly letters I wonder what events will be recorded. Good or bad days, I'll always keep your ever fresh memories before me, knowing deep down in my heart that in a short while we will be together again.

Every day I imagine what I think you would be doing at that particular moment and many a pleasant thought I have dreaming away the hours we had together. If it wasn't for those thoughts and dreams, I think I would go mad suffering the petty irritations the Japanese soldiers and to a slight extent, the Japanese civilians, deal out every day.

Also, the food is different to what we are used to. Added to this is the cold weather which, when all added up, means a fairly miserable life.

This week being the start of the New Year, I fervently hope that this year will see the conclusion of the war and also an enjoyable year for you and your parents.

News being scarce at this moment, I'll say Au-revoir and best of luck.

Love Fred xx

10th January 1944

Dear Nola,

Great news. On Monday evening the 3rd a second batch of letters arrived and included were two letters for two Australians. Although I never received a letter I feel happy because I know that they're on their way. The news in general was that things were more or less unchanged. The boys receiving their letters made me feel a little home sick and I'm hoping and praying that my letters will include a photo of you.

Well my love, apart from the news of letters, the only other news is that all the men had an injection against typhus as a precautionary measure.

The number of sick persons here is eight people, only one serious. Early in the week, a Dutchman died of pneumonia mainly through his own fault because he wouldn't take his medicine.

Thanks to God, we have amongst our midst, an American naval doctor who knows his work and does all he can for his patients. Without his knowledge I think that the sick rate would tremendously increase but thank God, it is not so.

Well my love, that concludes the news for the time being,

so until further news I'll say Au-revoir and best of wishes.

Love Fred xx

23rd January 1944

Dear Nola,

Having a few moments to spare I'll take the opportunity to pen you a few lines regarding the news of the past week.

First of all, I am in fairly good health and looking confidently towards the ultimate conclusion of the war.

Best of all my love, I received a message and vision of paradise. On the 21st I received a letter and photo from an angel whose name is Nola. If you only could imagine how welcome that letter and photo is. Now that once again I have your photo with me I'm not afraid to face any ill-treatment the Japanese can mete out to me. I am overwhelmed with joy to notice that you are looking the picture of health and I am more determined to arrive home again and continue the happy times we had together before we were so tragically separated.

The last news is that on Sunday evening the 23rd, 25 parcels for American prisoners arrived at the camp and later were issued to the different men. As these parcels were personal parcels from friends and relatives, the contents were in the nature of a surprise, but I can assure you, every article was a treasure in itself.

Well my love, that concludes the news for the time being, so I'll say Au-revoir and best of everything.

Love Fred xx

JAPAN'S WAR EFFORT WANES

30th January 1944

Dear Nola,

Having a few moments to spare before I retire, I'll take the opportunity to write the news of the past few days.

At present, I am working on the outside gang wiring motors and houses and work like that.

The last few days we were ordered to strip occupied houses of electric wiring as the wire was needed in Tokyo. If this news is correct, I feel sure that Nippon's reserved stocks are finished. Needless to say the news was rather cheering and I have convinced myself that this destructive war will arrive at a successful conclusion some time this year.

The Japanese civilians are realising that it is very improbable that Nippon will win this war, so they are beginning to be spiteful and commit childish acts against the prisoners.

When the Japanese have experienced a few heavy air-raids I think their attitude will change to fear and the treatment of the prisoners will change for the better. When this war is over, the Japanese authorities will have to give a detailed explanation regarding their treatment of prisoners of war.

Well my love, that covers the news regarding the events of local happenings so I'll finish this letter by remarking that I have enclosed the photo of an angel in a wooden photo frame made by an American sailor off the USS Houston. Every morning the first thing I notice when I awake is your photo and also the last thing I do before I sleep at night is say a short prayer for your health and speedy conclusion of this war.

Well my elusive girl, I'll conclude this letter by wishing you the best of health and happiness and with the kind thoughts of your mother and father before me, I'll say Au-revoir and sweet dreams.

Love Fred xx

6th February 1944

Dear Nola,

This week was full of good news because more letters and parcels arrived for the American prisoners-of-war.

Although the letters and parcels were for the American

prisoners, we were all cheered up because it meant that the letters and parcels were on the move.

The only other news worth relating was that we experienced a severe cold night which froze the water in the pipes, causing several to burst, one which supplies the camp, the result being no water up to the present time.

Apart from that news there isn't much more to say. The weather is cold, the Japs are spiteful and everybody is awaiting some decisive battle regarding the battle between America and Japan.

Well my love, that concludes the news for the time being so until next letter, I'll say Au-revoir and best of luck.

Love Fred xx

20th February 1944

Dear Nola,

With your photo before me, I have let my mind travel back to enjoy once again the wonderful memories of the happy times we had together. Many a laugh we had during a sunny Sunday afternoon and many a happy hour we spent together at one or more dance halls.

With those memories ever before me, I'm confident that I will be able to overcome any trial or tribulation that Nippon can offer me, and it is with a light heart that I look forward to a happy future with you.

> *A driving mind-set of the POWs was to not let those yellow bastards get us down – we will survive – no matter what!*

Well my elusive girl, there is only one interesting piece of news this week and that is; on Sunday 20th eight of the eleven officers left our camp, bound for Hakodate. Although the three officers left include Captain Zeigler, our commanding officer, and Captain Epstein our doctor, included in the officers that left, were Captain Campbell and Warrant Officer Vowels our two and only Australian Officers.

Well my love, that concludes the news, so I'll say Au-revoir and best of wishes to Mr and Mrs Caldwell and best of everything for you.

Love Fred xx

28th February 1944

Dear Nola,

Continuing from the previous letter, I can only say that this letter is as barren of news as the previous epistle.

Enjoying my usual good health and eagerly awaiting the day when this stupid war will be over and I am back once again with you.

In Ohasi, the weather is slightly cool, an average of 34° Fahrenheit and rapidly becoming warmer as the days go by.

The outstanding fact at present is that this mining village is the best fed in Japan and the rations which the Japs receive is very pitiful, so I can readily believe that the majority of the population are starving.

Well my elusive girl, I'm always thinking of you every day and often think of the enjoyable times we had together and I'm sure, of the many more enjoyable times we are going to indulge in after this war is over. So with these kind thoughts, I'll end this letter hoping that your father and mother are enjoying the best of health and happiness.

Love Fred xx

A Million Men

A million men in uniform

A million men to fight

A million men, a million guns

To prove that might is right.

A million human bodies

To suffer and to bleed

A million men in uniform

Consigned to cannon feed.

A million men to depart too soon

A million men to die

A million hearts will cease to beat

And yet no one knows why.

A million more men to take their place

A million for the cause

A million more are yet to fight

A war to end all wars.

6th March 1944

Dear Nola,

Yesterday, Sunday 5th, we received a load of American Red Cross parcels totalling 200, equivalent to one packet per man. The parcel was appreciated very much. American Red Cross clothing and shoes also arrived but at present the goods have not been issued.

Well my love, there isn't much in the way of news. The same average number of accidents in the mine, fatal or otherwise, the Japanese people becoming more and more irritable as their food and clothing rations decrease. As luck would have it, the prisoners are the best dressed and well fed of all the people in Ohasi and if a person thinks about it, he can't help seeing how ridiculous the whole system of Japan is.

There being no more news, my elusive girl, I'll end this short letter hoping that you are in the best of health and spirits.

Until next letter, I'll say Au-revoir and best of everything,

Love Fred xx

13th March 1944

Dear Nola,

At present the weather is very cold and snow is falling very thickly. During these days the snow has risen to a depth of three feet. Needless to say, all types of transportation are at a stand-still. When we proceed to work which is a distance of 1 $1/2$ miles, it is hard to say whether a person is walking on top of the road or on top of the fence skirting the railway line. Owing to the great depth and weight of snow many of the high tension electric power lines are down and all power and lighting is cut off. Naturally, work of all kind is stopped and this stoppage is a serious blow to Japan's war effort.

Well my love, apart from that news, there isn't any other news worth telling, so rather than bore you with a repetition of my daily routine, I'll end this letter wishing you the best of everything and the warmest of regards to Mr and Mrs Caldwell.

Love Fred x

26th March 1944

Dear Nola,

Having a few minutes to spare before lights out I'll pen down the few items of news which I have gathered. The weather has been warmer for the last few days which has enabled the Jap electricians the opportunities to repair the faulty power lines. Now that the mine has electricity once again, production is in full swing and the Japs are once again unwittingly wrecking things. Speaking to a few Japanese workmen, I was amazed when they grumbled that the mine was once again in full swing. Analysing the gist of their conversations, it appears that they are of the opinion that every delay in the war production means that the finish of the war will come quicker.

On the evening of 25th the new Japanese Colonel in command of the Hakodate Prison Camps, Colonel Imoto, addressed a gathering of us prisoners for 25 minutes in very fast faultless English. The gist of the lecture was obedience and good health. After listening to his speech and judging the man by his appearance, the general opinion was that the colonel was a gentle-man and honest person who would give everybody a square deal and severely punish anybody who misbehaved himself.

Well my love, there isn't much more I can write about, so I'll end this short letter by wishing you the best of everything, so until next letter, I'll say Au-revoir, and lots of love.

Love Fred xx

27th March 1944

Dear Nola,

With your ever-fresh memory before me, I'll try my best to make this letter as interesting as possible.

Today, Monday 27th, five American medical orderlies and one American army doctor arrived in this camp, after an exciting voyage from the Philippines Islands. According to their story, they had rather harrowing experiences. Not content with starving and beating the American prisoners, the Japanese even went as far as burying two men alive.

There was a group of four sick men lying down beneath a tree. A Japanese Sergeant ordered the men to rise and walk over to another group of men, only two of the men being able to rise. The Japanese ordered the other prisoners to dig two shallow ditches. The work completed, the two remaining sick men were thrown into the ditches and buried. Whilst the earth was being thrown in, one of the sick men struggled to a sitting position, so a Japanese officer threw a log of wood at him and ordered the rest of the dirt to be shovelled in. Feeling rose high amongst the remainder of the prisoners numbering approximately 120 men, but as there were approximately 50–60 Japanese with loaded rifles and machine guns, the men could only try to hold their feelings in check. Later in the afternoon, the prisoners were marched away to their camp and later separated. Whilst on the voyage to Nippon, one of the Japanese escorting cruisers was torpedoed by a submarine and sunk, otherwise the voyage was uneventful.

Well my love, the remainder of the news is only a repetition of previous news, so I'll conclude this letter by wishing Mr and Mrs Caldwell the best of everything and hoping that I'll be with you again in the near future.

Love Fred xx

8th April 1944

Dear Nola,

This week is rather barren of outstanding news. Yours Truly is in good health and ever looking at the photo of a beautiful angel. Night after night, whilst I'm in bed I dream of the wonderful moments we had together and when awake, I think of the good times we'll enjoy in the future.

Well my love, in Ohasi the routine is as usual, I'm working on the denshas, the average number of accidents occur daily with a few fatal accidents here and there.

The tobacco rationing is very strict. At present, it is one packet of cigarettes every three days. Every morning there is a queue of people, approximately a hundred yards long, and the early people receive the cigarettes.

Well my elusive girl, there isn't any more news worth writing, so I'll say Au-revoir and best of luck, and pass along my warmest regards to Mr and Mrs Caldwell and all your friends.

Love Fred xx

15th April 1944

Dear Nola,

Having a few minutes to spare, I'll use this opportunity to pen down the few items of news that have occurred.

Things in general are the same. The average number of accidents in the mine, the average number of people having sickness and all said and done, this week is no different from previous weeks.

The only outstanding news is that the Japanese

Commandant is to be replaced by another Japanese officer and the camp is changing over to Tokyo jurisdiction.
The change occurs on the 21st of this month and on the
20th the Hakodate Colonel, Imoto, is arriving at this
camp. Needless to say there will be an inspection and
speech by the Colonel.

Well my elusive girl, that concludes the news for the time
being so I'll end this short letter by wishing you the best of
every thing.

Love Fred xx

*PS: We receive the second issue of American Red Cross
parcels on the 14th and the parcels were welcomed very
much.*

22nd April 1944

Dear Nola,

Having a few minutes to spare, I'll take this opportunity to
pen the few items of news.

The only item of news is that the change over of
Command occurred on the 20th.

That day being yasme day, all the prisoners were congregated in the new barracks and lectured by the old Commandant of the POW camps, Colonel Imoto. The text of his speech was that he made several new orders regarding the betterment of our conditions as POWs and also an increase in food. The reason being he wanted the prisoners to carry back to their respective countries good impressions of Japan and Japanese treatment.

On the afternoon of the 22nd the actual changing over of the command from Hakodate to Tokyo administration occurred. A Japanese Major introduced the new Japanese Commandant of this camp, a 2nd lieutenant, and spoke to us about obeying their orders and keeping ourselves healthy. After that, the old Commandant spoke about how sorry he was to leave this camp etc.

Well my love, that concludes the news for the time being so until later, I'll say Au-revoir and best of everything.

Love Fred xx

29th April 1944

Dear Nola,

Having a few moments to spare, I'll take this opportunity to pen the few items of news.

This week has been no exception for accidents in and around the mine and the amount of bandages and medicine which is used in Ohasi is tremendous. I am at my usual routine, fixing their stupid denshas and wondering how they keep running.

The weather is rather warm at present and on one of the mountain sides, I saw monkeys for the first time this year. These monkeys belong to the tail-less type and are of medium stature, covered with short scraggy hair. The average height would be 4–5 feet. In winter, they live in the caves and eat roots. In summer they climb the trees and eat flowers, insects and fruit etc.

Well my love, that concludes the news for the time being, so until next letter I'll say Au-revoir and best of everything.

Love Fred xx

7th May 1944

Dear Nola,

At present the weather is rather warm and everybody is feeling rather languid.

I often think of the joyous moment we had together, during the warm nights of summer, so I wish and pray for the speeding of the finale of this war, so as we can be together again.

Well my love, things are more or less the same. The average number of accidents and the usual number of deaths.

Lately, the number of men called back into the army has been remarkable. Men are leaving the different shops every day and if the average rate continues, there will be only Koreans and prisoners left in this village.

Well my elusive girl, that concludes the news for the time being, so until next letter, I'll say au-revoir and best of everything.

Love Fred xx

14th May 1944

Dear Nola,

With your thoughts ever refreshing and your photo by my side, I'll pen the few items of news for this week's letter.

Yours truly is in the best of health and spirits and filling the hours with work (?) at the densha.

Lately, there has been three or four visiting Nippon officers inspecting the camp and prisoners, and according to the Japanese, the general opinion is that this camp is the second best camp in Japan.

The first camp is the allied officers' camp at a place named San Souci and this camp is the Japanese propaganda camp for the benefit of visitors, foreign or otherwise.

Well my love, there isn't anything further to add to this short letter so I shall say Au-revoir and best of everything to Mr & Mrs Caldwell and may all your wishes come true.

Love Fred xx

21st May 1944

Dear Nola,

I will try to relate the incidents of the past week and I hope you will not be bored too much.

The main item of news is the collapse of the mine.

The mine here is in a mountain range which rises to 750 metres, and the different working levels are, 350m, 450m, 500m, 550m, 600m and 700 metres. The ore is dropped down into shoots to 350m, where the ore is taken out by ore cars pulled by the Densha electric locomotives.

On the 18th, the ceiling of the 500m level fell into the 500m level and in parts, the floor of the 500m fell into the 450m. The exact number of killed and injured was never told, but the POWs who were working in the mine at that time estimate the casualties to be Nipponese: 17 dead, 25 injured; Koreans: 8 killed and 30 injured.

The causes of the falls are water filtering between the layers of rock, and the excessive dynamite blasting over the last few days.

Well my love, that concludes the news for the time being so I'll say Au-revoir and best of everything.

Love Fred xx

2nd June 1944

Dear Nola,

Having a few minutes to spare, I'll pen down the rather uneventful facts of the past week.

This week the weather has been fine and everybody is sun-tanned and looking fairly healthy.

Lately, there has been a rumour that 200 new prisoners are coming to Ohasi on the evening of the 20th of this month. I believe they are from Singapore so I expect to meet more Australian soldiers and perhaps a few personal friends.

Well my love, I am still working at the Densha and things in general are the same.

Every night I look at your photo, say a short prayer and then dream of the happy times we had together and whilst awake, I often think of the glorious times we will have after this war is over.

Well my elusive girl, I think that concludes the news for the time being, so until next letter, I wish you best of every thing.

Love Fred xx

7th June 1944

Dear Nola,

Today is Saturday and with a photo of a beautiful angel beside me it is natural that I should think about the wonderful times we had together.

If we were together, I would be preparing for an enjoyable evening at the Heidelberg Town Hall and looking forward to three or four dances with you. But my love, fate ordains otherwise and I am here in Japan instead of Melbourne, but I am confident that I will be with you by Easter 1945.

News in general is uneventful, so I will not bore you by writing the same routine sentences which are more or less in the other weekly letters so I'll end this letter with a prayer that your parents and yourself are in the best of health and spirits.

Love Fred xx

13th June 1944

Dear Nola,

Once again I sit down and pen the daily events of the past week. I'm sorry to say that this week has nothing of outstanding news, so I'll do my best to make the letter as interesting as possible.

At present the company has stopped production in the top half of the mine because of the dangerous condition of the mine. Owing to this part of the mine not operating, the prisoners are working outside the mine, carrying tree trunks from the mountain side down to the road.

Yours Truly is still filling in the time at the densha and patiently awaiting the finish of this war, so as I can be with a beautiful angel again.

Well my elusive girl, I think that concludes the news for the time being, so until further news, I'll say au-revoir and best of everything.

Love Fred xx

20th June 1944

Dear Nola,

Once again I'll write to the beauty of a girl far away. I hope that although the news is uneventful, the letter will not be boorish.

At present the weather is very mild and conditions are fairly good.

Since we have had the new Japanese commandant, there has not been any slapping of prisoners either by him or the guards.

I am working at the Densha as usual and the average number of persons have been injured so I will not bore you by a repetition of other weekly news, so I'll end this letter by hoping and praying for the day when we will be together again.

Best of regards to Mr and Mrs Caldwell and all your friends.

Love Fred xx

Ohasi Prison Camp 17-8-45
Back row (L-R): R. Drabble (WA), C. Hindes (NSW), J. Benson (NSW)
Front row (L-R): K. Edmond (WA), Fred Lasslett (Vic), F. Parker (NSW), F. Ward (NSW).

27th June 1944

Dear Nola,

With your photo before me, I have re-read the one and only letter I have received since I have been a POW, (March 1st 1942).

The more I regard your photo and peruse the letter the more thankful and amazed that such a girl as you should have any time for a person like me, but such is life.

Nothing unusual has happened here so I will not bore my elusive girl by repeating the usual news that happens every day.

I'll close this letter by wishing you the best of health and happiness and a very happy future.

Love Fred xx

4th July 1944

Dear Nola,

Today 4th July was celebrated in Ohasi by an air-raid scare. The actual bombing of the island was further south but the aircraft flew quite close on their journey over.

The Japanese inhabitants were quite panicky and for us prisoners it was rather a laugh. How the Japs will react when 500 aircraft are over-head dropping their messages of death, I think will be indescribable.

Personally I hope that only the harbour facilities and large industrial concerns are bombed, thereby saving much needless waste of women and children's life.

Well my love that concludes what little news there is so I'll say au-revoir and best of everything.

Love Fred xx

At this point, the lead pencil, which was getting fainter and fainter, ran out. So this ends the Letters to Nola.

The letters were never sent.

EPILOGUE

My last entry in my War Diary was the 4th July, 1944.

The experience at the POW Camp was fairly mundane over the next 12 months until the Americans dropped the atomic bomb on Hiroshima on 4th August 1945 and Nagasaki on 9th August 1945.

The following week we knew something exciting had occurred – the guards were gesticulating and shouting between themselves and acting not so aggressively to the prisoners.

I found out later from our Japanese person who was in charge of the Densha depot, that the Americans had dropped large bombs that had done a lot of damage around Tokyo. This Japanese person spoke little English, but kept me informed with a lot of news about the war. I cannot remember his name but he treated us as fellow workers and not as prisoners. Naturally, I did not write this down in my diary in case it was discovered by the Japanese guards.

Conditions at the camp were awash with rumours that the Allies were ready to attack Japan and also that Japan had surrendered. Imagine our surprise when one morning in September we woke up to find all the guards had disappeared. About 10am an American jeep arrived at the camp with American Naval Officers. They informed us that the war with Japan was over and that a military truck would transfer the American, English and Australian POWs to Manila.

Later that day we boarded the army truck with little luggage and taken to the port of Karmaiche and onto an American destroyer. That afternoon we left and eventually arrived at Manila (Philippines).

As we landed I looked over the Bay of Manila and was amazed at the sight of many Allied warships and hundreds of merchant ships. I was later informed that this was part of the invasion force on Japan.

When we disembarked a military vehicle took us to an American Army camp. Six of us Australians were billeted in an army tent with an American Army chap as our guide and instructor. After having a wash and tidy up we went to dinner for our first solid meal in three years.

Nobody knew what to feed us, so we joined the line of soldiers and received a roast meal of beef, potatoes and peas. We sat down at a table with our American friend and enjoyed the best meal I've enjoyed for many years, and finished with a cup of coffee.

When we went back to our tent we were presented with a large bar of chocolate and a cigar. It was funny, there were six Aussies smoking cigars with the American, and we were sure we were not upstaged by the American.

Later we went to an outside theatre to watch American films.

Next day we had a medical check-up. I was down to six stone, but otherwise healthy. We were interviewed by war criminal officers for information about Japanese atrocities against Japanese POWs. We were also issued with an Australian Army Pay Book with fifty pounds credit.

We stayed at Manila for a few weeks and were allowed leave from the camp to visit the city of Manila. We were warned to travel together in case of being robbed by the locals who were very poor due to Japanese occupation.

We were notified that we would be transported to Sydney, Australia, and later boarded HMS Speaker, a British aircraft carrier.

On board, we were supplied with blankets, shaving equipment, soap, towels and a duffel bag to stow our equipment. Also we were presented with an officer's waterproof jacket.

We had a smooth trip to Sydney and arrived on 15th October 1945.

In Sydney, we were processed at the Garden Island Naval Depot, where we were re-kitted in naval uniform. We had another medical check and were once again interviewed by War Criminal Officers for information about Japanese atrocities against POWs.

An excerpt from History of H.M.S. Speaker (http://www.navsource.org/archives/03/cve-40/speaker.htm):

PASSAGE DOWN SOUTH (30th September to 15th October, 1945).

Our visit to Manila was once again a trying one. Formidable was already in harbour attempting to get her load of passengers on board, but as it blew every afternoon and the camp was 15 miles out, a decision any morning to bring the men down to embark only got them there too late for calm weather. So we waited two days before we could get going. Even then we got away before Formidable!

All ex-POWs had steadily been improving in health and morale with the passage of time. The bunch we now embarked (all Australians), after a fortnight's rehabilitation, fitting of uniforms, etc., in Manila, and under an outstanding CO in Major R Newton, who had been with many of his men for four years and earned their affection and respect, were a really fine crowd. They readily took a share in the duties required, and were keen to join in the ship life.

The only thing we now had on our minds was the ship's appearance. None of us wanted to enter Sydney looking like

---

a bit of old iron as the result of our three months without a chance to paint. So we went full speed and found ourselves somewhere off Brisbane on a glorious calm morning with ten hours to spare. We stopped and in no time the stages were over the side, two boats were down and a mass of men, including 100 volunteers from the Aussies, were busy with paint brushes. By 1800 we were finished painting overall, having shot five sharks which were hanging around hoping for a meal. We got under way again, with a feeling of profound satisfaction which was confirmed when we steamed through the Heads, smart as new paint. Sirens hooted, ships cheered, motor boats followed us in and we felt once again we were in the public eye.

A week later I received a leave pass and train ticket to go home to Melbourne.

It was strange to walk along the street I live in and knock on the door and see Mum for the first time in 3 1/2 years. Mum burst into tears and so did I.

Pop told me that Nola had married. I was disappointed, but it was understandable after little contact for over three years of war. I tried to make contact with her, but she had changed address.

The following week I received a letter to proceed to a rehabilitation course for two weeks and then to HMAS

Cerberus (Flinders) where I was officially discharged.

Soon after that, I met Gwen Payne. We married in 1948, and enjoyed a happy marriage with four children for 52 years, until Gwen died in 2000.

Fred Lasslett

TO A SAILOR
AND A MAN

Somewhere a woman, thrusting tears away
Faces the future, bravely, for your sake
Toils on from dawn to dark, from day to day
Fights back her tears, nor heeds the other ache
She loves you, trusts you, breathes in prayer your name
Soil not her faith in you, by sin or shame.

Somewhere a woman – mother, sweetheart, wife,
Wait betwixt hopes and fears for your return
Her kiss, her words will cheer you in the strife
When death itself confronts you, grim and stern
But let her imagine all your reverance, claim
When base temptations scorch you with their flames.

Somewhere a woman watches – thrilled with pride
Enshrined in her heart, you share a place with one,
She toils, she waits, she prays, till side by side
You stand, side by side, when the battle's done
O' keep for her dear sake, a stainless name
Bring back to her a manhood, free from shame.

APPENDICES

IMPERIAL RESCRIPT

We, by grace of heaven, Emperor of Japan, seated on the Throne of a line unbroken for ages eternal, enjoin upon ye, Our loyal and brave subjects:

We hereby declare War on the United States of America and the British Empire. The men and officers of Our Army and Navy shall do their utmost in prosecuting the war. Our public servants of various departments shall perform faithfully and diligently their respective duties; the entire nation with a united will shall mobilize their total strength so that nothing will miscarry in the attainment of Our war aims.

To insure the stability of East Asia and to contribute to world peace is the far-sighted policy which was formulated by Our Great Illustrious Imperial Grandsire and Our Great Imperial Sire succeeding Him, and which We lay constantly to heart. To cultivate friendship among nations and to enjoy prosperity in common with all nations, has always been the guiding principle of Our Empire's foreign policy. It has been truly unavoidable and far from Our wishes that Our Empire has been brought to cross swords with America and Britain. More than four years have passed since China, failing to comprehend the true intentions of Our Empire, and recklessly courting trouble, disturbed the peace of East Asia and compelled Our Empire to take up arms. Although there has been reestablished the National Government of China, with which Japan had effected neighborly intercourse and cooperation, the regime which has survived in

Chungking, relying upon American and British protection, still continues its fratricidal opposition. Eager for the realization of their inordinate ambition to dominate the Orient, both America and Britain, giving support to the Chungking regime, have aggravated the disturbances in East Asia. Moreover these two Powers, inducing other countries to follow suit, increased military preparations on all sides of Our Empire to challenge Us. They have obstructed by every means Our peaceful commerce and finally resorted to a direct severance of economic relations, menacing gravely the existence of Our Empire. Patiently have We waited and long have We endured, in the hope that Our government might retrieve the situation in peace. But Our adversaries, showing not the least spirit of conciliation, have unduly delayed a settlement; and in the meantime they have intensified the economic and political pressure to compel thereby Our Empire to submission. This trend of affairs, would, if left unchecked, not only nullify Our Empire's efforts of many years for the sake of the stabilization of East Asia, but also endanger the very existence of Our nation. The situation being such as it is, Our Empire, for its existence and self-defense has no other recourse but to appeal to arms and to crush every obstacle in its path.

The hallowed spirits of Our Imperial Ancestors guarding Us from above, We rely upon the loyalty and courage of Our subjects in Our confident expectation that the task bequeathed by Our forefathers will be carried forward and that the sources of evil will be speedily eradicated and an enduring peace immutably established in East Asia, preserving thereby the glory of Our Empire.

> The 8th day of the 12th month
> of the 16th year of Showa.
>
> HIROHITO
> (Imperial Seal)
>
> Hideki TOJO, Prime Minister, and Concurrently
> Minister of Home Affairs and War Minister
>
> Kunihiko HASHIDA, Minister of Education
>
> Teiichi SUZUKI, Minister without Portfolio
>
> Hiroya INO, Minister of Agriculture and Forestry and
> Concurrently Minister of Overseas Affairs
>
> Chikahiko KOIZUMI, Minister of Welfare
>
> Michiyo IWAMURA, Minister of Justice
>
> Shigetaro SHIMADA, Minister of the Navy
>
> Shigenori TOGO, Minister of Foreign Affairs
>
> Ken TERASHIMA, Minister of Communications
>
> Okinori KAYA, Minister of Finance

Nobusuke KISHI, Minister of Commerce and Industry

Yoshiaki HATTA, Minister of Railways.

This Imperial Rescript was released by the Board of Information, December 8, 1941, and carried on the front page of all Japanese newspapers in the evening editions on that day. The above version was released in English in the Japan Times & Advertiser. Until September 1945, on the eighth day of each month thereafter throughout the war, the Rescript was reprinted in the papers as the solemn reaffirmation of Japan's war aims.

HMAS PERTH

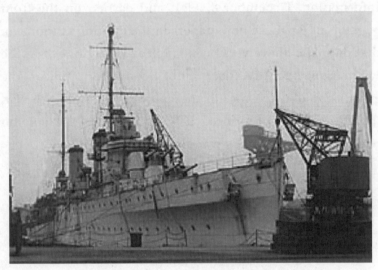

HMAS PERTH (1) (ex HMS AMPHION)

Details:

Type:	Light Cruiser (Modified 'Leander' Class)
Displacement:	6,830 tons (standard)
Length:	555 feet (water-line) 530 feet (between perpendiculars)
Beam:	56 feet 8 inches
Draught:	15 feet 8 inches
Speed:	32.5 knots
Propulsion:	4 Parsons geared turbines - SHP 72000
Laid Down:	26 June 1933
Launched:	26 July 1934 (Marchioness of Titchfield)
Armament:	8x6 inch guns 8x4 inch guns 4x3 pdr guns 8x21 inch torpedo tubes
Builders:	Portsmouth Naval Dockyard
Completed:	July 1936
Aircraft:	Walrus amphibian (of 9 Squadron, RAAF)

HMS AMPHION commissioned at Portsmouth on 15 June 1936. After trials she left Portsmouth on 18 July to join the 6th Cruiser Squadron with two Hawker Osprey aircraft embarked.

The cruiser arrived at Simonstown, South Africa on 3 October 1936 and spent the next two years as Flagship on the Africa station, based on the Cape of Good Hope and cruising as far north as Dakar on the west coast and Beira on the east. Her mid-commission refit was undertaken at Simonstown in the late autumn of 1937.

AMPHION departed Simonstown early in October 1938 and arrived at Spithead on 14 December, proceeding to Portsmouth the following day to pay off for a refit. Her Commanding Officer throughout the commission had been Captain R.L Burnett, OBE, RN.

The refit at Portsmouth Dockyard involved, among other modifications, the addition of a 'heavy' catapult to accommodate a Seagull V amphibion and the installation of modern twin 4 inch anti-aircraft mountings in place of the original old 4 inch guns.

Following agreement between the British and Australian Governments for the purchase of AMPHION for the RAN, it was decided to transfer the ship in 1939. Subsequently the cruiser HMAS ADELAIDE paid off and her crew, who were to man the new addition to the RAN, left Australia for the United Kingdom on 15 May 1939 in SS AUTOLY-CUS.

On 29 June 1939, the cruiser was commissioned in the RAN at Portsmouth as HMAS PERTH, under the command of Captain Harold B Farncomb MVO RAN. A highlight of the short period of peacetime service the ship was to envoy under the Australian flag was a visit to New York to represent Australia at the World's Fair. PERTH's stay at New York lasted from 4 to 16 August 1939.

Before the outbreak of war, it had been intended that PERTH would be sailed to Australia before the end of 1939. When war appeared imminent at the end of August the ship was in the West Indies. Pending the arrival of RN ships, she was ordered to protect oil tankers operating between Trinidad and Venezuela. For the next two and a half months PERTH carried out escort and patrol duties in the West Indies and Western Atlantic.

Late in November 1939 the ship passed through the Panama Canal and proceeded to Cocos Island with orders to fuel the Royal Canadian Navy destroyers OTTAWA and RESTIGOUCHE. At the end of the month PERTH returned to the Atlantic and proceeded for Kingston, Jamaica. Escort and patrol duties continued until early March 1940. The ship again passed through the Canal on 2 March 1940 and sailed for Sydney the following day. She secured alongside at Garden Island on 31 March.

Most of April was taken up by a refit followed by engine trials. On 5 May 1940, PERTH escorted the troopship QUEEN MARY that was joining Convoy US 3, the third convoy of Australian troops going to the Middle East. After briefly escorting the convoy in company with HMAS AUSTRALIA, PERTH returned to Sydney. Patrols and practice firings on the Australian east coast followed. On 6 June 1940 at Garden Island, Captain sir Phillip Bowyer-Smyth RN assumed command from Captain Farncomb. The following day, the flag of the Rear Admiral Commanding the Australian Squadron (RACAS), Rear Admiral John G. Grace was struck in HMAS CANBERRA and hoisted in PERTH, which was to be the Flagship of the Squadron for almost six months.

Until almost the end of November 1940, PERTH was engaged in patrols and escort work around Australia. On 27 November at Fremantle, RACAS transferred his flag from PERTH to CANBERRA. On 28 November PERTH left Fremantle as an escort for the seventh Middle East convoy, US 7. At different times, ships of the Royal Australian Navy, Royal Navy and Royal Indian Navy were in company as escorts during the voyage. Aden was reached on 12 December and the ship's Walrus aircraft was landed to work from shore. Two days later the ship left Convoy US 7 to assume duty as escort to a southbound convoy.

On 16 December PERTH arrived at Aden where she re-embarked her aircraft the following morning and then proceeded to take over as escort of a northbound convoy. The cruiser and the vessels under her charge some having detached and gone ahead arrived at Suez on 23 December.

The ship proceeded through the Suez Canal and after a short stay at Alexandria she took up duty in the Mediterranean as a unit of the 7th Cruiser Squadron (PERTH and RN ships). During a visit to Suda Bay Crete, on 1 January 1941, PERTH's aircraft was landed and subsequently deployed as courier and on other base duties.

The month of January was occupied mainly with patrols and also included transport of troops to Crete and Malta. Whilst in port at Malta, PERTH was damaged by a near miss in an air raid. In February the ship's work was again principally patrolling. From 9 to 20 February PERTH was in dock at Alexandria for partial repair of the damage sustained at Malta the previous month.

In the first half of March the ship took part in the reinforcement of forces in Greece by taking two trips with troops from Alexandria to Piraeus. She resumed patrol duties on 19 March. During the night of 28–29 March, PERTH played a minor role in the Battle of Matapan, in which the Italian Navy lost three cruisers and two destroyers as against the British losses of five Fleet Air Arm aircraft.

Patrol work was resumed after the Battle of Matapan and continued into April. Late in the month PERTH participated in the evacuation of troops from Greece to Crete. On 29 April 1941, PERTH's aircraft was shot down off Suda Bay, but its crew of three was rescued by destroyer. Patrols and convoy escort duties occupied the ship during May, since being damaged at Malta, PERTH had several times escaped damage in attacks by German aircraft, but on 22 May enemy aircraft succeeded in damaging the ship by a near miss.

During a stay at Alexandria from 24 to 28 May urgent repairs were carried out. On 28 May, PERTH sailed for Crete to assist in the evacuation, being attacked en route by a German aircraft but fortunately escaping damage. During the return from Crete with 1188 passengers aboard PERTH the convoy was attacked five times and on 30 May the ship was hit by a bomb in a boiler room. Two cooks, two sailors and nine passengers were killed and the boiler room was put out of action. The ship was later badly shaken by several very near misses. Alexandria was reached on 31 May and PERTH remained there until 25 June undergoing repairs. Late in June, PERTH was engaged in operations off Syria against Vichy French forces. These included bombardments of shore positions and patrol work. On 15 July the ship, which was to be relieved by HMAS HOBART, proceeded to Alexandria for return to Australia. She sailed from Alexandria for Australia on 18 July.

On 12 August 1941, PERTH arrived at Sydney and the following day moved to Cockatoo Dockyard for an extensive refit. Acting Commander Charles R. Reid RAN assumed command on 1 September 1941 and was relieved by Captain Hector M.L. Waller DSO and Bar RAN on 24 October 1941. After completion of her refit on 22 November PERTH was engaged in exercises from 24 to 30 November and then sailed for Auckland. She carried out patrols, escort duties, exercises and manoeuvres during December 1941 and January 1942, visiting New Caledonia and New Guinea.

On 14 February 1942, PERTH sailed for the Java Theatre. She arrived on 24 February at Batavia, where Japanese aircraft attacked her during that day and the next, without sustaining damage. PERTH sailed on 25 February for Surabaya in company with four Royal Navy ships. On 26 February the ship departed Surabaya in company with the Dutch cruisers DE RUYTER and JAVA, the cruisers USS HOUSTON and HMS EXETER, two Dutch destroyers, four US destroyers and HM Ships JUPITER, ELECTRA and ENCOUNTER and proceeded along the north coast or Madura Island. During the night of 27–28 February an eleven ship ABDA (American, British, Dutch and Australian) force engaged Japanese forces in the disastrous Battle of the Java Sea, from which only PERTH and HOUSTON survived.

HMAS PERTH and USS HOUSTON arrived at Tandjong Priok on 28 February after the day and night actions off Surabaya. Unfortunately stocks of fuel were low and PERTH could only receive 50% of full stowage. Preparations were being made to destroy all warehouses and harbour installations, so the opportunity was taken to embark any stores that might prove useful. Orders were received to sail in company with HOUSTON and the Dutch destroyer EVERTSEN through Sunda Strait to Tjilatjap. PERTH and HOUSTON cast off at 1900 hours making a signal at the same time to EVERTSEN to precede them out of harbour. Not having received the orders to sail, she was told to obtain the necessary orders and follow as soon as possible. The harbour entrance was passed at 1900 hours and a course set for Sunda Strait. HOUSTON was stationed five cables astern of PERTH.

At 2306, a vessel was sighted about five miles close in to St Nicholas Point. When challenged she proved to be a Japanese destroyer and was immediately engaged. Shortly afterwards, other destroyers were sighted to the north and the armament split so as to engage more than one target. During the action a large number of enemy destroyers attacked from all directions, and due to the large number of enemy ships attacking, it was impossible to engage all targets at once and some were eventually able to close to a very short range.

The Japanese warships were protecting an invasion convoy of approximately 50 ships that effected a landing in Banteng Bay, Java.

Little damage was caused to PERTH until the very end of the action. At about midnight it was reported that very little 6" ammunition was left, so Captain Waller decided to attempt to force a passage through Sunda Strait. He ordered full speed and altered course for Toppers Island. PERTH had barely steadied on course when she was struck on the starboard side by a torpedo. Captain Waller gave the order to prepare to abandon ship. A few moments later another torpedo struck just ahead of the first hit, and the Captain gave the order to abandon ship. After five or ten minutes a third torpedo struck well aft on the starboard side. This was followed shortly afterwards by a fourth torpedo, which hit on the port side. The ship then righted herself, heeled over to port and sank about 0025 on 1 March 1942.

USS HOUSTON was still fighting although badly on fire. She was hit by torpedoes and sank shortly afterwards rather closer inshore. A Japanese report gave the Japanese losses as 'one mine-sweeper and one transport of convoy sunk and several vessels seriously damaged'.

Most of PERTH's crew abandoned ship between the second and third torpedoes, but it is doubtful if any of the boats were successfully launched. Many Carley rafts and wooden life rafts were launched. During the abandon ship operation PERTH was under fire from several destroyers at close range and many hits were scored and casualties caused. Many were killed or wounded in the water by the explosion of the last two torpedoes and by shells exploding in the water.

At the time of her loss PERTH's ship's company totalled 681, comprising 671 Naval personnel, six RAAF personnel (for operating and servicing the aircraft) and four civilians (canteen staff). Three hundred and fifty Naval personnel (including Captain Waller) and three civilians did not survive the sinking. Those who did numbered 328 (324 Naval, three RAAF and one civilian).

Four Naval personnel died ashore without having been taken prisoner. A further 106 men died in captivity (105 Naval, one RAAF). Four sailors were recovered from captivity in September 1944 when they were among prisoners-of-war rescued after the sinking of a Japanese transport. After the end of hostilities 214 men (211 Naval, two RAAF and one civilian) were repatriated to Australia.

Source: Naval Historical Section, Canberra

DIVING SITE

Today the wrecks of the HMAS Perth and USS Houston can be explored on their final resting sites in Banten Bay on the Eastern approach to the Sunda Straits. These two sites are only accessible by experienced divers due to the depth of the wrecks and the strong currents that are common in this area. Visibility can also present some real challenges especially on the USS Houston, which lies in soft silt.

The USS Houston sits in about 30 metres with the deck level at about 17m. Diving this wreck you must be luck to get the right conditions as the soft silt sediment of the ocean floor here can be whipped up by the strong currents, bringing visibility down to almost zero. However, if you are lucky enough to dive this site when visibility is okay, you will be rewarded with the sight of a well pre-served heavy cruiser complete with 8 inch guns.

The HMAS Perth, located 3 Nm from the USS Houston, is a much more reliable dive.

Sitting in 36 metres of water with deck level at about 21 meter, the sediment here is sand, resulting in less sediment and better visibility. Again much of the ship is intact, however having been hit by many torpedoes there is heavy hull damage. In fact there is one point where a large hole has been blasted from port to starboard allowing you see right through the superstructure of the ship. The 6″ guns of the Perth are still mounted and make a spectacular sight.

THE END

ABOUT THE AUTHOR

Fred Lasslett lives in a suburb of Melbourne, Victoria.
An energetic 93 year old, he spent Christmas day playing cricket
with his well-loved family.

Our people

Fred's a hero 50 years on

by JODI PINE

WHEN Fred Lasslett stood in front of a Japanese firing squad waiting to die, he did not know how to fear ... and that almost certainly saved his life.

The Japanese thought the fearless man was possessed by a God and set him free to become a prisoner of war for three years.

He also escaped death during the war when he, with a group of other Australian sailors, put out a fire on a merchant ship.

And for that, more than 50 years after the event, Mr Lasslett, now [illegible], has been awarded the Malta George Cross in appreciation of his heroism.

The merchant ship was moored at Valetta Harbour when, during an air raid, a bomb went down its funnel into the boiler room and started the fire.

It was not until after the fire was out that Mr Lasslett was told the harbor could have been wiped out because the ship was loaded with ammunition.

"I think I aged 10 years when they told me that," he said.

"A lot of strange things happened that day. A 2000-pound bomb landed in a toilet on the pier, and luckily didn't explode. The top was sticking out and I think that deterred anyone needing to go."

Mr Lasslett joined the Naval Reserves in 1935 and four years later was called for duty and joined HMAS Perth.

After three years of convoys to Malta and the Mediterranean, the Perth sank in the Sunda Straits off Indonesia.

For 11 hours the survivors, Mr Lasslett one of them, clung to a rubber dingy carrying the dead and the wounded, before a Japanese destroyer rescued them.

"There were about 800 of us and we were taken to a rundown theatre, where we were held," Mr Lasslett said.

"I'd had enough and tried to escape but I was caught and confronted by the Japanese general and his four-foot sword, which looked to me like 14 feet.

"I was then taken out to the wall to be shot, but all I could think was what a beautiful day it was. That's when they decided not to shoot me because I was showing no fear, either that or they thought I was mad."

For three years Mr Lasslett ate three rice balls and a cup of seaweed a day. When the war was over the POWs were released and sent off with the Americans.

FRED Lasslett with his Malta George Cross medal. Picture: COLIN STUCKEY

Former POW gets ready for his 'last hurrah'

By CLAIRE HALLIDAY

When Fred Lasslett was called up to join the navy in the early days of World War II, he felt excited, thinking it would be a chance to see the world. He says today that the reality of being in a war zone never crossed his mind.

"I was just a lad," Mr Lasslett said last week.

Now, in what he says will be his "last hurrah", Mr Lasslett, 8[illegible], is globe-trotting again. On Friday, as part of a 19-strong tour group, he will be on a plane bound for Turkey.

"I've always wanted to go to Gallipoli, especially for Anzac Day. They reckon the atmosphere — particularly the dawn service — is electric," he said.

It will no doubt evoke memories of his wartime experience. "You always felt in danger," Mr Lasslett said. "Especially when you were getting dive-bombed. You could hear the planes coming a mile away. It was a real piercing scream and then you'd see the bombs coming down."

In 1941, in a major battle over the defence of what was then known as Java, Mr Lasslett's ship, the HMAS Perth, was sunk. The first torpedo came mid-ship.

"Then we got another one and the captain yelled 'abandon ship'," Mr Lasslett said. "I took a deep breath and jumped overboard."

Clinging to a raft, he managed to help some injured colleagues to safety. They were in the water for about six hours before they were collected by a Japanese destroyer.

When Mr Lasslett escaped from his first prisoner of war camp, he was put before a firing squad before being spared at the last minute — something he attributes to Japanese superstition. "I didn't really flinch when they had me in their sights. I found out later that the Japanese way of thinking is that if you're very brave or very silly then the gods are in you and they can't attack you."

Eventually transferred to another camp in Japan, Mr Lasslett was a POW for three years.

"When they dropped the atomic bomb we woke up one morning and all the guards had disappeared. After about an hour an American truck came up and they told us what had happened. They took us away. I'd been living on rice and seaweed for three years. I went down from 11 stone (70 kilograms) to about 6½ stone (41 kilograms)," Mr Lasslett said.

Despite his ordeal of hard labour, meagre rations and regular beatings, Mr Lasslett said he never suffered ill effects in his postwar life. "As soon as I had a couple of Aussie beers I was right."

There will be beers on Anzac Day, too — a day Mr Lasslett says has always been special. "You meet your mates — some of them you only see once a year — and of course we win the war all over again." Only this time, at Gallipoli.

Fred Lasslett, who survived a Japanese firing squad, with his portrait as a 20-year-old navy recruit.

something about me

HEIDELBERG resident Fred Lasslett has been around the world — and he wouldn't live anywhere but Heidelberg.

Born in 1918 and the president of the RSL District Board, Mr Lasslett talks about his life journey.

I joined the HMAS Perth in 1940, arriving in the Mediterranean Sea in December during World War II.

I fought in the battle of Matapan, fought fire on an ammunition ship in Port of Valetta Harbour, Malta, and evacuated defence personnel at Crete.

When I first got called up, I thought it was a big adventure.

But during the actual battles, you knew who your

in late 1941 and went into the defence of Indonesia in early 1942.

shown while facing the firing squad.

I was kept in isolation for

forbidden wireless news to other allied commanding officers.

But that wasn't the only move.

I was transferred to Japan until the end of the war and worked in an iron-ore mine at Hokadati.

On return to Melbourne at the end of the war, I married my late wife, Gwen, in 1948.

We moved to Heidelberg because I appreciated the country look it had at the time.

For my service in the war, I have been awarded an Australian Service Medal, Australian Defence Medal, Australian War Medal, 1939-1945 Star, 1939-1945 African Star, 1939 Pacific Star and the Cross of Malta Medal.

Be Published

Publishing through a successful Australian publisher. Brolga provides:
- Editorial appraisal
- Cover design
- Typesetting
- Printing
- Author promotion
  - National book trade distribution, including sales, marketing and distribution through Macmillan Australia.
  - International book trade distribution
  - Worldwide e-Book distribution

For details and inquiries, contact:
Brolga Publishing Pty Ltd
PO Box 12544
A'Beckett St VIC 8006

Phone: 0414 608 494
admin@brolgapublishing.com.au
markzocchi@brolgapublishing.com.au
ABN: 46 063 962 443

AUSTRALIAN WAR DIARIES

Fred Lasslett

ISBN 9781922036551		Qty
	RRP AU$24.99	.....
Postage within Australia	AU$5.00	.....
	TOTAL* $_____	
	* All prices include GST	

Name:..

Address: ....

....

Phone:...

Email: ....

Payment: ❑ Money Order ❑ Cheque ❑ Amex ❑ MasterCard ❑Visa

Cardholders Name:...

Credit Card Number: ....

Signature:..

Expiry Date: ....

Allow 21 days for delivery.

Payment to: Marzocco Consultancy (ABN 14 067 257 390)
PO Box 12544
A'Beckett Street, Melbourne, 8006
Victoria, Australia
Fax: +61 3 9671 4730
markzocchi@brolgapublishing.com.au